2011 – 22

D1030088

Work Smart

STRATEGIES FOR CAREER SUCCESS

JENNIFER BALAISHIS
York Region District School Board

REINA CHIDIAC
York Region District School Board

JANE COUGHLAN
Toronto District School Board

JESSICA PEGIS
GENERAL EDITOR

MICHELLE DE BRAUX
Toronto District School Board

MARC EMOND
Educational Consultant

JOAN TIMMINGS
Peel District School Board

ALAN WASSERMAN
York Region District School Board

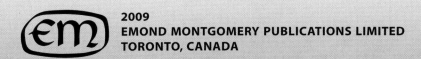
2009
EMOND MONTGOMERY PUBLICATIONS LIMITED
TORONTO, CANADA

Emond Montgomery Publications Limited
60 Shaftesbury Avenue
Toronto ON M4T 1A3
http://www.emp.ca/school

Printed in Canada.

We acknowledge the financial support of the Government of Canada through the Book Publishing Industry Development Program (BPIDP) for our publishing activities.

ISBN 978-1-55239-267-6

Publisher
Anthony Rezek

Marketing manager
Christine Davidson

National sales manager
Lindsay Mascherin

Managing editor
Jim Lyons, WordsWorth Communications

Production editor, copy editor, & additional writing
Tanjah Karvonen

Image researcher & permissions editor
Paulee Kestin

Cover designer & illustrator
Darren Hick

Interior designer & compositor
Tara Wells, WordsWorth Communications

Indexer
Paula Pike, WordsWorth Communications

ADVISORY PANEL

Emond Montgomery Publications Limited would like to thank the following reviewers for their contributions to the development of *Work Smart: Strategies for Career Success*.

Rob Wilson
Peel District School Board

Agostino Carbone
York Catholic District School Board

Adele Castriota
York Catholic District School Board

Tanya Fraser
Trillium Lakelands District School Board

Maurice Guzzo
Toronto Catholic District School Board

Kelli Watson
Ottawa Carleton District School Board

CONTENTS

WELCOME TO WORK SMART

Work Smart is your guide to career exploration and planning. It will help you build your knowledge of different opportunities in the world of work, practise your work-related skills, and boost your confidence about your options for the future. The learning you do in this course isn't just for finding the right job—it's for life.

But first, here's a guide to getting around the book.

Open It Up

Part opening pages show you what you are expected to learn in that part of the book. Together, all four parts of *Work Smart* make up the expectations for your Career Studies course.

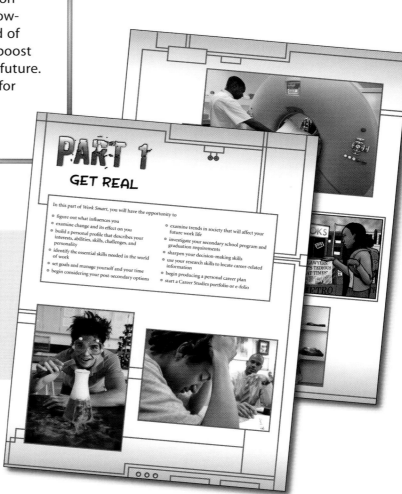

Chapter Openers

Each chapter in *Work Smart* starts off with a real-life situation that illustrates a big idea in the chapter. You will be invited to consider how this idea relates to your own life and career exploration. This will also help you identify the focus of the chapter.

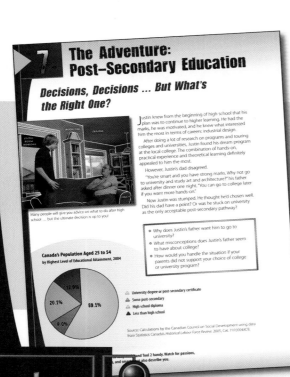

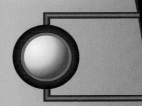

Use Tools

In *Work Smart*, you'll get the chance to use tools to figure out who you are, what employment opportunities are out there, and what occupations or careers might be the best fit for you. Your teacher will provide you with Tools 1, 2, and 3 to use with the text. Look at Tools 1, 2, and 3 often to see how much you have learned about your own potential career path. Directions for use appear right on the tools. Check the lights at the beginning of each chapter—they provide you with tips on how to proceed.

> Keep Tools 1, 2, and 3 handy while you choose a culminating activity. If you discover more information about yourself by doing this activity, add that information to the appropriate tool.

Do the Search

When you see this icon, you will be asked to do some web research around a specific issue or field of work.

Take the Test

When you see this icon, you will be asked to take a test or quiz to see how much you know about yourself and the world of work.

Get Support

When you examine the culminating activities on pages 153–160, you will see this icon. This indicates that you may ask for help or feedback from your teacher.

Get the Meaning

Find the meaning of bolded words in the margin glossary.

> **work smart**
> use your passions, preferences, and smarts to find out which career would best suit you; then work in a way that maximizes the new strategies that you have just learned

Get Wise

The Wise Words margin feature presents inspirational quotations to think about. They may help you consider different ways to think about the world of work and how you will fit into it.

Use the Pictures

Work Smart uses a lot of visuals to convey information and work advice. You're on the right track if you look at the pictures first.

Career Coach

Work Smart includes a graphic novel–style feature in every chapter called Career Coach. This feature offers advice on preparing for your future by making the right choices at school, learning how to motivate yourself, getting an interview, and so on. A unique feature of the Career Coach is an invisible mentor (guide) who gives advice in many forms.

Real–Time Resumé

This feature makes you the coach! You will read about real-life situations young people encounter while finding their way in the world of school and work. Some of these situations are quite tough. What advice will you give? The Reality Check panel gives you additional information on each situation.

Profiles

Work Smart features stories of real young people in real-life training and work situations. These profiles will answer some of your questions and may even inspire you in your own career exploration. You will have the opportunity to think about the young people profiled and compare their experiences to your own.

Go Smart

Work Smart features interactive activities that allow you to apply the skills and information that you have learned—anything from interviewing someone who is self-employed to creating a blog entry that explains where you might be headed based on your self-knowledge.

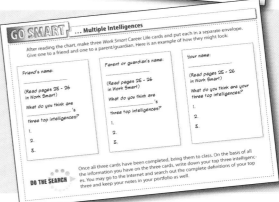

Portfolio

Your Career Studies portfolio or e-folio helps you organize the key material that you either create or learn about. Your teacher will distribute various line masters during the course, and these may be good additions to your portfolio. Your portfolio should also house your Tools and the results of any self-assessments.

Sum It Up

Use the chapter summaries at the end of each chapter to find the big ideas and strategies to move forward in your career exploration and in your Career Studies course. The lights prompt you to pause and check your own progress. Red means review, green means go!

This chapter introduced you to the following ideas:

1. Everyone has internal and external influences that shape who they are and where they are going.
2. It is important to dream and to have goals. Both are required for career planning.
3. A job that pays a lot of money is not necessarily the job that will make you the most satisfied or the happiest.
4. Attitude plays an important part in finding the right career path, in accepting and even embracing change. A positive attitude can go a long way!
5. Jobs of the future will require a creative mix of training, education, skills, and lifelong learning.
6. Certain jobs are better suited to introverts while other jobs are better suited to extroverts. Knowing your personality type will help you decide.
7. A portfolio or e-folio is an effective way to organize and keep track of all that you have learned about yourself, your skills, where you are now, and where you are going.

PART 1

GET REAL

In this part of *Work Smart*, you will have the opportunity to

- figure out what influences you
- examine change and its effect on you
- build a personal profile that describes your interests, abilities, skills, challenges, and personality
- identify the essential skills needed in the world of work
- set goals and manage yourself and your time
- begin considering your post-secondary options
- examine trends in society that will affect your future work life
- investigate your secondary school program and graduation requirements
- sharpen your decision-making skills
- use your research skills to locate career-related information
- begin producing a personal career plan
- start a Career Studies portfolio or e-folio

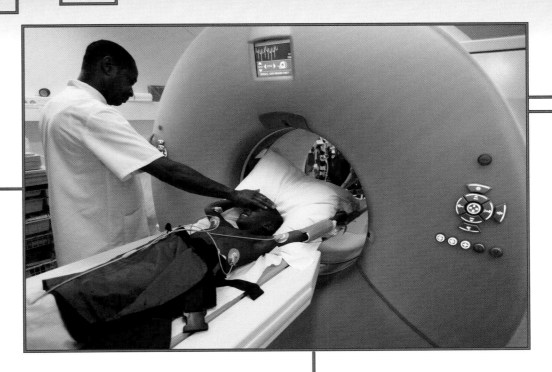

▶ 1 You Have Options

Where Are You Now?

A new semester means new courses and a big workload. Balancing a social life, committing to sports, activities, a part-time **job**—you name it!

Talk about choices and commitments. Talk about stress!

And in Grade 10, a required Career Studies course, among other things. You can be sure there will be assignments. More importantly, there will be some deep questions to contemplate:

- Where are you now?
- Where are you going?

job
position that has specific tasks and duties at a specific location

career
summary of all your education, paid work, volunteer experiences, and activities of interest to you

Start by taking a deep breath, looking around, listening to the sounds, and feeling the ground beneath you. Easy, right? Probably some thinking going on too, but those thoughts will likely change by the time you finish reading this paragraph. There is just so much to consider. And then it hits you.

Mulling over the really big question, "Where are you going?" isn't easy.

Just ask Melanie.

WHERE AM I GOING? WELL ... I HAVE A MILLION DREAMS ABOUT BEING AN ARTIST, ... WHAT KIND WILL I BE? A PAINTER ... MAYBE A PHOTOGRAPHER ...

THEN THERE WAS WHAT MS. JANICKI SAID LAST WEEK ABOUT HOW I'M DOING WELL IN MATH AND DID I EVER THINK OF A **CAREER** IN THAT AREA — THAT THREW ME ...

NOW I CAN HEAR MY MOM TALKING ABOUT PICKING A CAREER THAT WILL PAY THE BILLS AND LET ME SAVE SOME MONEY TOO ...

THEN THERE WAS THAT MAGAZINE ARTICLE I READ LAST NIGHT ABOUT ARTISTS HELPING KIDS THROUGH ART THERAPY. THEY USED THEIR PASSION TO HELP OTHERS: NOW THAT'S COOL.

WHAT WAS THE QUESTION AGAIN?

Melanie's influences: Which influences are **external** (outside her)? Which influences are **internal** (inside her)?

Tool 1, Tool 2, and Tool 3 are your tools for this course. They will help you focus your career planning. Keep them safely in your portfolio.

There's a great deal to consider when answering the big question, "Where are you going?" It's one of the most complex questions of all—definitely not one that can be answered in a few minutes. It takes some people years to figure it out. Reading *Work Smart* may not help you do that tomorrow, but it will help you focus your energies and streamline the process.

GO SMART ... Influences on Your Decisions

1. a) Think about which factors influence you in your life right now (both internal and external). Jot them down in list form on a piece of paper.

   b) Are there any other influences you can think of that Melanie has not considered? Share your ideas with a partner.

2. a) How do the influences on your list affect the decisions and choices you make now? List some of your possibilities for the upcoming weekend, for example, things you are planning to do—both personal and school-related—and some things you want to do. Think about all the factors involved, such as "My parents will influence which social events I attend" or "My strengths in sports will influence which teams I make this year."

   b) Which influences do you see having the biggest impact on your decisions for the future? Give one reason for each.

From Dreamer to Goalie

Melanie has lots of dreams. Dreams are necessary, but dreaming is just one part of knowing where you are going. The other part is knowing how to set **goals** for yourself.

goals
what you want to achieve for yourself

See if you can spot the dreams and the goals in the illustration below.

1. GOTTA BE A STAR!

2. I'M GOING TO TRY ONE NEW RECIPE A WEEK TO IMPROVE MY SKILLS.

3. ME, A ROADIE! TALK ABOUT BLISS.

4. SOMETHING TO DO WITH KIDS — THAT'S WHAT I'D LIKE.

5. TOMORROW I'M SUBMITTING MY RESUMÉ TO THE SOURCE.

6. BEING A CHEF IS MY DESTINY.

7. I AM GOING TO DO SOMETHING IMPORTANT TO PROTECT THE ENVIRONMENT.

8. IF I COULD DJ MY WAY THROUGH COLLEGE, THAT WOULD BE GREAT.

9. OK, I'VE NOW GOT THREE VOLUNTEER AGENCIES TO CHECK OUT BY FRIDAY.

10. TAKING THE STAIRS INSTEAD OF THE ESCALATOR ... EVERY SINGLE DAY.

How did you do? Did you spot the goals among the dreams?

What influences you? What gives you satisfaction? What kind of person are you?
Throughout this chapter, start using Tool 1.

Goals are specific, realistic, and time-sensitive. They also express an intention to act. Dreams, on the other hand, help to start the process of thinking and planning. They are clues about your interests—your passions. However, they are not in themselves actions or intentions. **Aspirations** are your goals and dreams mixed into one. That's a powerful combination that gets you on the way to achieving something great!

aspirations
strong desire to achieve something great; your goals and dreams mixed into one

If you only dream, you won't get anywhere with your career plans. If you plan before you dream, you may find your goals uninspiring. So you need to do both.

Here's one more tip: pay attention to what you are doing today. Noticing when your dreams, goals, and actions align is a powerful way to tap into where you are really going in life. These activities will help you do that.

GO SMART ... Goal-Setting Basics and a Life Timeline

1. a) Think about a small personal goal for the rest of today. It might be something like tidying your room. (Remember: goals represent an intention to act.) Now think of a school goal— for example, attending all classes today. Next, complete the line master distributed by your teacher with a goal for today, tomorrow, this week, and this month. Keep in mind that once you have determined your goal, you will need an action plan. What steps will you take to achieve this goal?

   b) Now transfer your goals into your personal agenda. If you must achieve your goal by a certain time, write down the time—for example, "Get to the gym by 4 p.m." If your goal is something you intend to do but don't need to schedule, simply write it down as your daily goal. At the end of the day, cross it out if you achieved it.

2. Make a timeline of your life using the line master distributed by your teacher.

   a) Record your dreams and goals as you remember them in the past, as you see them now, and as you imagine them in the future. Use your answers to Activity 1 to help you complete the Today and Future sections. Then record what you remember doing, are doing now, and may be doing in the future.

   b) Are there any points in your life when your aspirations align with your actions? How does it feel when they do? How does it feel when they don't?

   c) After responding to part b), what clues can you identify about your future—where you might be in 10 years? Circle them on your line master.

Your Timeline

	Childhood	Today	Future
My dreams and goals	o o o	o o o	o o o
What I'm doing	o o o	o o o	o o o

What Choice Are You Making Now?

Back to those questions:

- Where are you now?
- Where are you going?

Did you know that these questions are related? Where you are now will affect where you go, and where you think you're going will affect what you do today. As you read the profiles below, think about which style of getting from "here to there" seems most like you.

Alex Today

Age: 16

"What's hot?"

Alex lives for the moment. She always has lots of ideas and no fear about acting on the good ones. Her current desire to go to a beach for March break has inspired her to organize a trip to Mexico for her grade. When she thinks of something she likes, she tries to make it happen.

Charlie Mellow

Age: 16

"Today's special"

Charlie is good with his hands. He knows this because he has been taking apart, rebuilding, and fixing engines since he was small. He prefers automotive and math classes at school and works part-time at the local garage. He thinks that by following his passions and working to integrate them into his life, he will be in good shape for the future.

Miriam Choosy

Age: 15

"Need to decide"

Miriam can see herself working as an emergency room doctor down the road. She has wanted to be a doctor since her first visit to emergency. She makes choices today about courses, completing her school work, and doing volunteer work that will contribute to her goal of becoming a doctor.

Guy Future

Age: 15

"Healthy, please"

Guy sees himself as a future professional soccer player. He trains, eats right, and listens to his coach daily as if he were already a professional athlete. He thinks that acting like a professional soccer player now will ensure that it happens in the future.

GO SMART ... Decision Making

1. Choose the student—Alex Today, Charlie Mellow, Miriam Choosy, or Guy Future—who most closely reflects your thinking when considering decisions about the future. Where are you on the continuum? Your teacher will distribute a line master to help you with this activity.

2. Write one paragraph (use a scenario above as an example) outlining your thinking about one of your goals or dreams.

3. Join with classmates who see themselves on a similar point on the continuum. In your group, list the pros and cons of your preferred decision-making style. Share your results with the class.

OUR HERO WANTS TO TRAVEL OUT-OF-PROVINCE TO VISIT HIS COUSINS. JASPER HAS A PART-TIME JOB AND HE'S SAVED FOR THE TRIP. HOWEVER, HE ALSO LOVES STYLISH CLOTHES. ONE EVENING, AFTER SHOPPING FOR COOL CLOTHES, HE CHECKS IN WITH HIS FRIENDLY ATM MACHINE ... AND DISCOVERS SOMETHING AWFUL.

WOULD YOU BELIEVE THIS BALANCE! I'M NOT GOING TO HAVE ENOUGH FOR THE SUMMER TRIP! HOW COULD I HAVE BLOWN THIS MUCH CASH?

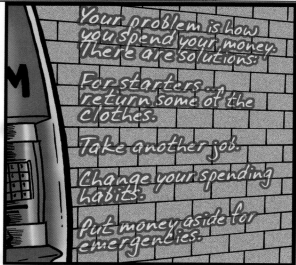

Your problem is how you spend your money. There are solutions:

For starters ... return some of the clothes.

Take another job.

Change your spending habits.

Put money aside for emergencies.

A FEW WEEKS EARLIER

COOL JACKET! MUST HAVE COST A FORTUNE BUT TOTALLY WORTH IT.

$200

Next time you spend, consider all of the things that you could spend that money on. Then choose the most important one to you.

C'MON—THIS CONCERT'S GOING TO BE EPIC. YOU'RE THE ONE WITH THE PART-TIME JOB— YOU CAN AFFORD IT!

NOPE, I'M NOT IN. THOUGHT ABOUT IT, AND I'M GOING TO SEE MY COUSINS NO MATTER WHAT.

1. IF YOU EARNED $500 AT A PART-TIME JOB, WHAT WOULD YOU PLAN TO DO WITH THE MONEY? EXPLAIN.

2. CREATE A PLAN THAT COULD HELP YOU MAKE GOOD DECISIONS WITH YOUR MONEY. YOUR PLAN COULD BE IN THE FORM OF QUESTIONS TO ASK YOURSELF BEFORE MAKING A PURCHASE, OR SOME OTHER FORMAT THAT'S EASY TO REMEMBER — FOR EXAMPLE, AN ACRONYM.

The Satisfaction Factor

Regardless of what you do now or in the future, you will always be making choices. Some of these will be academic; some will be economic; some will be personal; and some will be a mixture of all three.

How can you determine if you chose well? One way will be to evaluate how much satisfaction you ultimately experience from your choices.

When it comes to career planning, some people feel there's only one way to spell satisfaction.

What is it?

ALTERNATIVE ALTERNATIVE ALTERNATIVE
ALTERNATIVE ALTERNATIVE ALTERNATIVE
ALTERNATIVE ALTERNATIVE ALTERNATIVE
ALTERNATIVE ALTERNATIVE ALTERNATIVE
ALTERNATIVE ALTERNATIVE ALTERNATIVE
ALTERNATIV**CHOICE**LTERNATIVE
ALTERNATI **CHOICE** LTERNATIVE
ALTERNATIV LTERNATIVE
ALTERNATIVE ALTERNATIVE ALTERNATIVE
ALTERNATIVE ALTERNATIVE ALTERNATIVE
ALTERNATIVE ALTERNATIVE ALTERNATIVE

a choice among alternatives

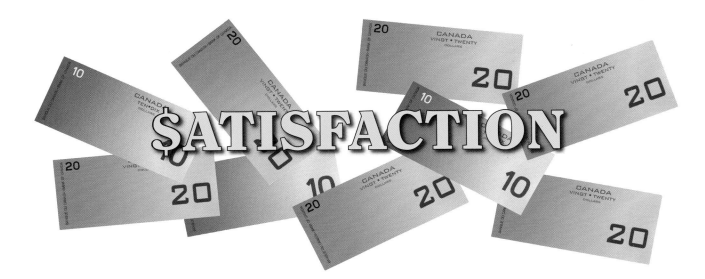

After all, a career that makes you lots of money will let you buy comfort, security, and freedom. You'll be able to spend the money on yourself and your loved ones, and what could be bad about that? But it's not quite that simple.

What if you were making lots of money but you hated the time you spent earning your salary? How much satisfaction would you have then?

One way to approach this dilemma is to investigate *which part of you* experiences satisfaction. Try this self-analysis:

- Which part of you has been with you the longest? Describe it.
- Which part of you doesn't change? Describe it.

The part of you that lasts is the part that experiences true satisfaction. Satisfaction doesn't come from the things that command your attention at any given moment. Instead, it comes from being drawn to something. In other words, satisfaction is active—it's not the thing; it's how you feel and what you're doing when you are focused on it.

Wise Words

"You can't have everything, and everything has a cost."
—*Penny Hopkins,*
Vice-President, Jobmatics

Happiness and income in economically advanced nations

Country	Happiness Ranking	Income Index (makes the most money)
Switzerland	1st	4th
Denmark	2nd	19th
Canada	3rd	16th
Ireland	4th	48th
Netherlands	5th	24th
United States	6th	1st
Finland	7th	31st

Happiness is one aspect of satisfaction. What does this chart tell you about wealth and happiness in general? Do these statistics surprise you? Why or why not?

Wise Words

"I think a lot of times it's not money that's the primary motivation factor; it's the passion for your job and the professional and personal satisfaction that you get out of doing what you do that motivates you."

—*Martin Yan, chef*

Ireland: Forty-eighth in income, but fourth in happiness. Go figure.

GO SMART ... Assessing Satisfaction

1. Think of areas in which people are satisfied—for example, material, social, intellectual, and spiritual. Using some or all of these categories (and including any of your own), complete a chart that illustrates examples of satisfaction in each category.

Satisfaction Table

Area of Satisfaction	Example
Material	○ Earning a lot of money ○ Having all of the new "toys" (electronics, clothing)
Social	○ Being popular with peers ○ Being loved by family and friends

2. Rank the importance of these areas of satisfaction and write a paragraph to justify your first choice.

3. Alone, or with a partner, write your own definition of satisfaction. Share it with the class.

4. Satisfaction is tough to achieve because life is really unpredictable. If you were to lose one thing or person today that would most affect your satisfaction, what would it be? How would you deal with it? Journal your response.

DIAL UP YOUR HEART AND FIND YOUR CALLING

So if satisfaction comes from meaningful work, what is meaningful work and where do you find it? Fortunately, doing what you love means being able to take advantage of opportunities that match your deep interests.

Jackie spent ten years as a "rock musician." Both her older brothers were well-known musicians. She toured, wrote songs, recorded music, and was offered record deals. She went so far as to get a music engineering degree. It was not her true calling, however, and she felt a sense of emptiness. She had also done yoga and meditation since her early teens.

After teaching an informal class to some friends and music colleagues, Jackie knew she had come across her life's calling. She closed her guitar case, took a book-keeping course, and set out on a business plan that would earn her a living spreading the practice of yoga and meditation to others. She committed to her life's passion, and never looked back.

Being a musician just wasn't Jackie's calling. Being a yoga instructor was.

FIND YOUR SATISFACTION, FIND YOUR ATTITUDE

Getting a great job is sort of like going to school. Even if you "have to," you can choose the attitude you bring. At school, you choose electives, sports, and extra-curricular activities. You also choose how you act in each of these situations. At a job, the stakes are even higher. All things being equal, the employee who smiles and brings a sense of joy to work is more likely to excel than the employee who doesn't.

What if you don't care or feel it's not cool to care? Realize that it is your own experience that you are neglecting when you don't care. If you don't care, it's your life—everyone else, friend or foe, can just walk away. But you can't.

GO SMART ... Finding Your Calling

Alone or with a partner, create your own definition of "calling." What words are associated with finding one's true calling? Think about your dreams, goals, actions, emotions, and values as you create your definition and word list.

The Crystal Ball: Job Trends for the Future

Now that you've examined the nature of satisfaction, you need more details about the world of work itself. After all, working in some capacity is important after graduation.

- What might some new future industries be?
- What career areas will be hot? Will they suit you?
- Can you really figure out what to study today?

baby boomers
people who were born during the post–World War II baby boom between 1946 and the early 1960s

longitudinal
repeated observation or examination of a set of subjects and variables over time

Of course, the business of forecasting job trends is not a science—it's really about making the best educated guess. Business analysts do studies, including **longitudinal** ones that take years to generate information, and then guess what happens?

Baby boomers are aging and instead of raising families, they are looking for products to ward off old age.

The picture shifts again. The economy might go up or down. The demand for certain skill types might shift in response to technological discoveries. There might even be a major shift in the composition of the population. Within a few brief years, for example, consumers in Ontario became much less concerned about baby food and more interested in protein shakes and vitamin supplements. Any ideas why?

The aerospace industry will also provide a wide range of high-tech jobs in the future.

Many jobs in health care will require a lot of high-tech knowledge, such as the use of MRI machines.

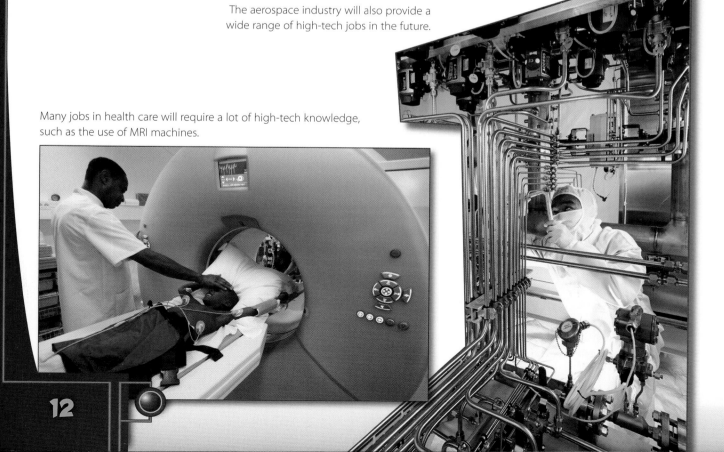

On the pages that follow you will find information about what business analysts think working in Ontario will look like from 2010 to 2015.

Where do you think you will fit in? Examine the lists of career areas and **occupations** on these pages. Do these jobs reflect the direction you would like to go in? Remember: these are the top jobs only. You may not find your calling here. The first list is labour market information from the Ontario Ministry of Education and Training, 2004–2009.

occupation
general title given to a group of similar work roles and skills (e.g., engineers)

Projected Job Creation by Occupation

1. Professional and technical services (except teaching and health care)
2. Manufacturing and processing
3. Health care
4. Management
5. Elemental sales and services
6. Services
7. Skilled trades
8. Sales
9. Transportation equipment, operations, installation, and maintenance
10. Clerical
11. Teaching

Here's another list. This one comes from Human Resources and Skills Development Canada. These are new and emerging industry sectors in the economy. Do you see yourself anywhere on this list?

Emerging Industry Sectors in the Economy

1. Aerospace
2. Environment
3. Gaming
4. Multimedia
5. Tele-health
6. Tele-learning

Did you notice anything? "Jobs of the future" require post-secondary education; a creative mix of training, education, and skills; and lifelong learning. Are you getting ready?

tionullam zzrit luptatu erciduisl utpatum dolestrud magnim nim ex eu faccum estion ut inibh eum elet.

Great job opportunity!

Looking for an Internet Specialist … producing and updating websites for clients, providing tech support to users through phone calls, site visits, and email. Must have software programming certification, problem-solving skills, ability to interact with customers. Participate in creation, editing, and distribution of technical documentation and training materials. Love of Penelope Trunk's blog an asset. Think it's you? **Email contact@iamsothisjob.com**

Unt utpat. Endrera esequipit alit adionse nisisit alisi. Acipit lorem zzriuscin hesit wisi. Ming eugue dolor si et laor alipo

San vel veli alit. ulla et l com mol alis

Lesti ing e num lut nit exero dolor strud ciduis min h faccu

THE WORK SMART INDEX

Length of time people are at their first job:
9 months

Number of different types of jobs the average person has during their lifetime:
7

Percentage of people actually working within their university/college major:
30

Percentage of first-year post-secondary students who change courses or drop out:
60

Percentage of jobs that will emerge in the service sector (see page 13) in 2009 and beyond:
75

Average number of years an employee stays at a given company:
5

Average yearly salary for a sales manager:
$87,580

Average yearly salary for a graphic designer:
$38,390

TOP 5 INDICATORS OF POOR POST-SECONDARY DECISIONS

- ☹ Avoiding making any decisions
- ☹ Course hopping (moving around from one course to another)
- ☹ Setting self up for failure by taking on something you are not ready for
- ☹ Taking a year off to postpone your next step
- ☹ Thinking some opportunity will just show up

Top 5 Reasons Why High School Students Choose Courses

1. "My friends are doing it."
2. "An easy course, what else?"
3. "Cool teacher."
4. "Parents made me."
5. "I'll need this course down the road."

THE PERSONALITY FACTOR: INTROVERT OR EXTROVERT?

Understanding which kind of work would give you satisfaction also depends on your personality type. **Introverts**, for example, can't be around people all the time—it drains their energy. **Extroverts**, by contrast, recharge by being around people. Have a look at some of the introvert jobs below from Lawrence Shatkin's *200 Best Jobs for Introverts*.

introvert/extrovert
how you get energy; an introvert recharges by being alone and reflecting quietly; an extrovert recharges by being around people and having conversations

Some Fast-Growing Jobs for Introverts*

1. Hazardous materials removal workers
2. Tile and marble setters
3. Animal trainers
4. Landscapers and groundskeepers
5. Brick masons, block masons, stonemasons
6. Heating, air conditioning, and refrigeration mechanics and installers
7. Sound engineering technicians
8. Roofers
9. Environmental science and protection technicians, including health-care technicians
10. Plumbers, pipefitters, and steamfitters

* with the highest percentage of workers aged 16–24

Animal trainer is a fast-growing job for introverts.

GO SMART ... Jobs for Extroverts

1. Research ten jobs you think an extrovert would like. Start by figuring out what aspects of a job would attract an extrovert. Post your list on a class bulletin board.
2. What specific aspects of a job would make you happy? Think about it for a few minutes. Write down your list of five things on your own and then share your list with your partner. Add your list to your Career Studies portfolio (see pages 17–18).

DO THE SEARCH

ENERGY ○ ● ● ● ●
MONEY ○ ○ ● ● ●

REAL-TIME RESUMÉ
I'm working my hardest ... why am I so unhappy?

Amal has always been known as smart, ambitious, and caring. In between school work, she volunteers and has a part-time job at the public library.

She also never slows down.

If her part-time hours decrease at the library, Amal runs over to the mall to pick up extra shifts at the cinema, grabbing a few tacos and fries on the way for dinner. She made her 40 hours of community service months ago but continues to volunteer at the Humane Society—two bus rides away—because … well … she loves animals.

However, Amal isn't happy. She's short-tempered with her family and she barely sees her friends. And to top it all off, she's gaining weight, which is really stressing her out. She's never had to watch her weight before.

One night, Amal gets a call from her friend Aaron—one of the most straightforward friends she has. Although Amal is feeling pretty low riding the bus home after 8:00 p.m., she answers her cellphone. Usually, she wouldn't. This is what she hears:

"What's up with you, girl? You haven't been online since forever. Everybody's wondering about you. You need to get a little balance in your life."

YOU BE THE COACH

You and your friends are Amal's friends. Your job is to help her regain *balance* in her life. You will do this in a group coaching session where you present your information to Amal. Remember: you really care about Amal and want to see her happier.

DO THE SEARCH ▶

REALITY CHECK

Your teacher will distribute support material for this activity. In the meantime, here is some information for you to consider:

● To enhance wellness, satisfaction, and happiness, it is important to treat your physical and emotional health, as well as your social and career aspirations, as equal priorities.

● There are proven ways to manage stress—talking to other people who care about you, reducing workload, exercising, making nutritional changes, reflecting on your own feelings, and so on.

● Satisfaction and happiness come from how you feel when you are doing the right things for you.

Me: Today and Tomorrow ... My Career Studies Portfolio

Have you ever been asked to place your work into a portfolio before? Why do you think keeping your work might be worthwhile?

Over the next few months, you are going to learn a lot about yourself, your personal interests, and your career interests. So creating your own **portfolio** (or **e-folio**) is a great way to keep all this learning at your fingertips—for you to reflect on quietly or show to someone important. Portfolios and e-folios can help you plan, monitor, and reflect on your learning.

portfolio

tool used to organize and maintain personal, academic, and/or career-related credentials and evidence of accomplishments

e-folio

electronic portfolio; an e-folio is a great way to save your work and update it frequently in cyberspace

GO SMART ... Portfolios and E-Folios

1. With a partner, spend five minutes searching for these key terms using a search engine and count how many schools are using portfolios or e-folios. Write down the names of the schools and where they are located.

2. Now spend some time noting the organization and appearance of the different portfolio formats, both paper and electronic. Write down three characteristics of the portfolios you looked at that appealed to you and state the advantage of each one.

DO THE SEARCH

THE PORTFOLIO ADVANTAGE

Portfolios are found in all stages of life and work. You can use them to

- keep your best work ready to present to a potential employer at a job interview
- show an apprenticeship committee the products you've made
- bring to a co-op education interview
- get into a high school program at another school
- apply to college or university with evidence of what you have done
- apply for scholarships or awards.

Portfolios also showcase your areas of strength, your talents, and your developing skills.

Portfolios can house photos of your favourite creations or the real thing!

INTO THE PORTFOLIO ...

Here are some assignments that you could place in a portfolio or e-folio. You and your teacher will discuss these options and you will have some choice. Don't forget to make your own suggestions as well!

DO THE SEARCH

- results from your self-assessment surveys and assignments
- results from cool career searches that have caught your interest—the ones you want to know more about
- high school subjects you are taking now and subjects you want to take (your course plan)
- your resumé(s) and cover letter(s)—different ones for different reasons
- letters of recommendation from teachers or people you have volunteered or worked for
- activities that you do in school and outside school—and new ones you want to try
- awards you've won—and other honours you would like to achieve
- your best work from Grades 9 and 10—what you are really proud of
- personal data and materials important to you now and in the future
- a "Me: Today and Tomorrow" statement of who you are and who you will become; what you value—today and tomorrow
- songs you have written, business ideas you have, role models who make you think

ANYONE WANT TO BE AN E-FOLIO MANAGER?

If your Career Studies class decides to use e-folios, you may find that they require some managing. One idea is to have a small group of students take on the role of e-folio managers.

The e-folio managers can help the rest of the class in various ways—for example, by giving short workshops on formatting and adding sound files, images, and videos; or by helping students use presentation software or create spreadsheets for self-assessment results. The e-folio managers can also help classmates personalize their e-folios, to make them as creative and original as possible.

Read the Summary on page 19. Are there any ideas you are unsure of? Are there any skills you need to practise? If so, go back and review them.

IT'S AN E-FOLIO UNIVERSE

Here are some ideas to try to make the most of your e-folios:

- Approach your school about giving your Career Studies class a section on their website. Your Career Studies class can display portions of your e-folios, including your class section, your teacher's name, your photos, and some of your class's best work.

- Begin a careers blog where other students come for advice. You could share what you are learning and maybe help them learn strategies to search for careers, such as, "How do I become a children's storybook writer?"

Ultimately, your portfolio or e-folio will demonstrate evidence of your learning, your ability to use your skills, and your potential—an important part of your career journey.

Wise Words

Starting from now, commit to the idea that your portfolio or e-folio holds everything you need to continue learning about where you are today and where you could be tomorrow.

This chapter introduced you to the following ideas:

1. Everyone has internal and external influences that shape who they are and where they are going.
2. It is important to dream and to have goals. Both are required for career planning.
3. A job that pays a lot of money is not necessarily the job that will make you the most satisfied or the happiest.
4. Attitude plays an important part in finding the right career path, in accepting and even embracing change. A positive attitude can go a long way!
5. Jobs of the future will require a creative mix of training, education, skills, and lifelong learning.
6. Certain jobs are better suited to introverts while other jobs are better suited to extroverts. Knowing your personality type will help you decide.
7. A portfolio or e-folio is an effective way to organize and keep track of all that you have learned about yourself, your skills, where you are now, and where you are going.

Confident that you are ready to move forward?
Then go to the next chapter.

19

2

You On Purpose

Jeffrey and Clara's Good Advice

Hey, sis, how goes it? Shouldn't you be studying or something?

Nah, exams are done. Good thing, too. Now I'll have a chance to think about things.

What do you mean, Clara? You aren't thinking of quitting, are you?

Well … I hate my courses and I'm not doing well at all.

No way. I just read in my course stuff that architect is one of the most overrated jobs, so maybe you're on to something.

(laughing) You may be right. But listen: you take that careers course seriously, OK, Jeffrey? All that stuff about looking at your interests, skills, values, what you're good at, can really go a long way when you do it right. I thought it was the same thing over and over. And the portfolio? I didn't even keep it—now I don't remember any other careers I would have liked. I was so sure about architecture.

Hey, you know … I am actually paying attention. You got to keep your options open. We just learned that about half of university and college students change their majors after first year. I guess maybe the careers they choose aren't really what they expected them to be.

All I know is that I don't want you to have as rough a year as I've been having. So I'm glad you're taking it seriously. Because now I really am thinking of switching and it won't be easy, especially with my grades.

Keep in the game, sis. You can figure this out.

Pretty smart for a 15-year-old … See ya.

JOBS WITH MYSTIQUE
- Advertising executive
- Architect
- Attorney
- Chef
- Chiropractor
- Clinical psychologist
- Medical scientist
- Non-profit manager
- Physician
- Police officer
- Real estate agent
- Small business owner
- Teacher

- Why does Jeffrey decide to tell Clara that her chosen path might be overrated?
- What happened to Clara? Why do you think it happened?
- What is the main idea that Clara is trying to convey to Jeffrey while he is still in high school?
- After talking with his sister, how do you think Jeffrey is feeling?

Some jobs have a certain mystique. They seem very important for society or glamorous. However, these jobs involve a lot of hard work. Why do you think people are attracted to them? What could be the downside?

Keep Tool 1 handy. Watch for passions, preferences, and smarts. You will have the opportunity to add a lot more information to Tool 1 in this chapter.

Change: The Only Constant?

What's the difference between change that's fun and change that's hard? One word: control. Most people like change when they initiate it. But how do you handle change when you don't control it? How do you stop fearing the unknown? How do you regain control over your current situation—maybe even over your life?

Enter **attitude**: something you *can* choose. Deciding to look at change from the optimistic (positive) side can bring

- excitement rather than fear
- growth instead of boredom
- confidence, not desperation!

Think *possibility* when change comes knocking. Change, your constant companion, will help to build your personal life and career in ways that you may not have ever dreamed possible. So how do you *do* that?

attitude

way of thinking and feeling about something or someone that shows your true opinion

With the right attitude, you can handle just about any change or new challenge.

GO SMART ... with Change

Practical Career Advice from Career Specialist John Krumboltz

1. Choose *one* statement here that rings true with you. Show how this statement explains your current career ideas and/or work experience. You may develop a short dialogue; create a short comic strip; draw an abstract picture; compose a poem; or design a graph explaining how this statement fits *you and where you are today*:

   - You have experienced pressure to choose a career.

   - You want to take action toward a career you are interested in, and not just sit and talk about it.

   - You follow up on leads that are suggested by people you have come in contact with.

   - Even with very limited experience, you do the very best work you can.

   - You are led to learning about and experiencing a possible career path through unplanned events, meeting someone, or reading an article by chance.

2. When you are finished, share your creative expression or story with some of your classmates. Analyze your classmates' experiences. Find two similarities and one difference between your stories. Write down these three ideas and give them to your teacher so that he or she can compile the ideas before a whole-class discussion.

Now is the time to begin using Tool 1 to match up the information found with Tool 2. If anything clicks, be sure to note it.

21

Me Choose a Career?
Are You Kidding?

Lots of students think that taking Career Studies is a pointless exercise. Perhaps you feel that choosing a career now makes about as much sense as choosing the clothes you might wear ten years from now.

However, maybe you're buying into some career choice myths, and not the realities. Do you think you are?

Wise Words

"The best way to make your dreams come true is to wake up."

—*Paul Valéry, French poet and philosopher*

Wise Words

"I think that my career had changed more dramatically than any of them. Most of my classmates had remained in engineering-related fields and some worked for pure chemical companies. My career sort of took a quick u-turn somewhere and I ended up both in politics and then in publishing. Could I have planned that or thought that? No, but thank goodness there is some mystery in life."

Paul Godfrey, chemical engineer turned politician turned publisher of the Toronto Sun turned CEO of the Toronto Blue Jays

The Myths	The Realities
• Ignore an unexpected event; it will throw off your plans.	• Get excited about unplanned events opening up your eyes to new opportunities.
• Choose a career early. That way you have lots of time to build up to it.	• Keep your options open always and forever. The world of work is fast-paced, so careers can change quickly too.
• Try not to make mistakes—hide from them!	• Make mistakes! They teach you about you! You get to see what you are made of and where you need to grow.
• Go after a job or career that you have the skills for.	• Get the job first and develop and learn new skills on the job.
• Always hold on to your beliefs.	• Sometimes your beliefs can hold you back and sabotage your growth.
• To be truly successful in your career, you must put it first.	• True success is a balanced life; your career, along with fun, family, friends, health, and money are all a part of that life.

GO SMART ... Career Myths

1. Ask your parents, guardians, or family friends to tell you a myth that they held when trying to choose a career. What was their reality check? Bring their ideas back to the class to share.

2. When Paul Godfrey said his career took a "quick u-turn," what did he mean?

How Do You Picture Your Career Adventure?

Now that you've looked at the myths and realities about choosing a career, try to let go of any preconceived notions you've had up to now. Go back to a time in your mind when there was no pressure but you were still drawn to doing certain things with your life. Take a few moments to recall that time. Then do these activities.

GO SMART ... Dream Career

Complete activities 1–5 to develop the ideas for your own career adventure. Then draw or create your own visual symbol for that adventure: is it a path, a sailboat, a flower garden, a computer, a soccer game, a tree, or a film, or something else?

1. Using point-form notes or a graphic organizer, tell the story of the career or careers you dreamed about when you were young, no more than 10 years old. If the idea of these careers—even one of them—still makes you happy and you still talk about it, then write down how this career still meets your personal needs and interests. Here are some questions to think about:

   - What did you value as a child?
   - Who influenced you?
   - What natural abilities did you have?
   - What was important to you about growing up?

When I grow up, I am going to be a …

2. When you daydream about the future today, what dream careers still come to mind? Write down your answer in sentences or share your ideas with a class-mate or friend. Ask that person to take notes while you discuss your ideas. Here are some questions to inspire your discussion:

   - What are the common themes or main messages about these dream careers?
   - What do you value about these careers?
   - Which parts of your personality seem to be important in these dream careers?
   - What pastimes do you have now that cross over into your dream career?
   - What barriers to having this career can you foresee?
   - What is important to you about the people working in your dream career?
   - What skills do they share with you?

GO SMART ... Dream Career (continued)

3. Create a community career genogram by interviewing family members, potential mentors (people who support you in your career development and achievements), and family friends.

   - What careers do they have or did they have?
   - How have they influenced your career interests?

   The career genogram looks like a family tree; however, it extends the meaning of family to include all important people who may have influenced your career ideas.

4. Using the following headings as a guide, pull out the main ideas and common themes from your stories and career genogram. You may also use your career adventure symbol (page 23) to help you organize your ideas. For example, if your career journey is a garden, each subheading could be seen as a flower growing at different rates at different times.

   - **Interests** (what you like—what your passions are) `TAKE THE TEST`
   - **Abilities** (what you're naturally good at)
   - **Skills** (what you have learned how to do)
   - **Personality** (the total you—are you introverted or extroverted?) `TAKE THE TEST`
   - **Influences** (which messages speak to you the most)

   - **Values** (what you truly believe in) `TAKE THE TEST`
   - **Pastimes** (what you like doing in your spare time)
   - **Challenges** (opportunities to grow in a new way)
   - **Aspirations** (your dreams and your goals mixed into one)

   Under each category, be sure to write down how those things are "you" at school, at home, with your friends, when you volunteer, or in your dream career. Your chart might look something like the one below. (Your teacher will distribute a line master.) You don't have to fill your chart out all at once. Take some time to think about the categories.

	At school or work	At home	With my friends	Volunte
Interests				
Abilities				
Skills				

5. Think of a time when you learned a skill that was really hard at first. However, as time went on, you got really good at it. How might this new skill become part of your skill set for your future career?

---

interests
what you like; something that attracts you—e.g., a book, a film, a superhero, an issue

abilities
something you do naturally; your talents and aptitudes—e.g., singing, running, using numbers or languages easily

skills
something you have learned or studied—e.g., playing the piano, speaking another language, leading a group discussion, using a computer

personality
your "self" that you build over time; the total of your physical, mental, emotional, and social characteristics

influences
anything or anyone that contributes to the way you think, and challenges or supports the decisions you make

values
your core beliefs; what drives you

challenges
opportunities to grow and to test abilities in a demanding but exciting way

Multiple Intelligences: Nine Ways to Express Your Brilliance

TAKE THE TEST

Howard Gardner is an educational psychologist who is interested in how people learn. In the 1980s, he started to think that people aren't born with a single intelligence. Instead, he thought, people must have at least seven intelligences that they use to learn new knowledge and skills.

Gardner's theory is now famous and is known as the multiple intelligences (MI) theory. Since that time, Gardner has added two more intelligences. Although everyone has some strengths in each intelligence, people usually prefer to rely on their strongest intelligences when they learn.

When you use your preferred intelligence, your self-esteem and your enjoyment in learning increase because you feel like you are learning "naturally." Knowing your different intelligences is another part of understanding yourself and undertaking your career adventure.

Do your career interests match your type of intelligence?

Intelligence	Description	Possible Careers
Verbal-linguistic	Word smart	Journalist, writer, TV broadcaster, comedian, editor, translator
Mathematical-logical	Math smart	Computer technician, banker, tool and die maker, engineer, scientist
Visual-spatial	Image smart	Graphic designer, landscaper, fashion designer, pilot, interior decorator
Bodily-kinesthetic	Body smart	Actor, athlete, personal trainer, builder, nurse
Musical	Music smart	Songwriter, singer, sound engineer, musician
Interpersonal	People smart	Teacher, public relations personnel, CEO, human resources manager
Intrapersonal	Self smart	Psychologist, artist, small business owner, author
Naturalist	Nature smart	Gardener, farmer, environmentalist, veterinarian, wildlife rehabilitator
Existential	Deep smart	Clergy, philosopher, spiritualist, humanitarian, poet

Danielle Di Vincenzo of Uxbridge always loved physics and astronomy. She decided to start her own science-based business called antiMatter. Danielle has also been an activist for animals and the environment since her teens, so that was important in her business plan. She now sells environmentally friendly and cruelty-free science-related gifts, clothing, and paraphernalia across Ontario. Danielle feels that her strongest intelligences are mathematical-logical and visual-spatial.

Danielle's interest in astronomy led the way to a small business.

GO SMART ... Multiple Intelligences

After reading the chart, make three *Work Smart* Career Life cards and put each in a separate envelope. Give one to a friend and one to a parent/guardian. Here is an example of how they might look:

Friend's name: _____ *(Read pages 25 - 26 in Work Smart)* What do you think are _____ 's three top intelligences? 1. 2. 3.	**Parent or guardian's name:** _____ *(Read pages 25 - 26 in Work Smart)* What do you think are _____ 's three top intelligences? 1. 2. 3.	**Your name:** _____ *(Read pages 25 - 26 in Work Smart)* What do you think are your three top intelligences? 1. 2. 3.

DO THE SEARCH

Once all three cards have been completed, bring them to class. On the basis of all the information you have on the three cards, write down your top three intelligences. You may go to the Internet and search out the complete definitions of your top three and keep your notes in your portfolio as well.

Your Learning Style

TAKE THE TEST

Your learning style represents your preferred sensory experience when learning. Visual learners like to see or read information. Auditory learners like to talk and listen. Kinesthetic learners like to jump in and just do it. Many people are a combination of two styles.

Check out the What You're Doing Now chart.

Teaching a friend how to use his new digital camera.

What You're Doing Now

What You're Doing	Visual	Auditory	Kinesthetic
Operating your new portable music player.	Read instructions.	Listen to store clerk explain.	Just figure it out.
Going to visit a new friend at his place.	Go to a map website.	Call him on your cellphone for directions over the phone.	Follow your instincts—you kind of know the area.
Cooking a meal for someone you like.	Follow the directions at a gourmet food website.	Call up a close friend who's a great cook.	Taste as you go.
Teaching a friend how to use his new digital camera.	Write out the instructions.	Explain it to him over tea.	Demonstrate and let him try.
You'd say . . .	I see what you mean.	I hear what you are saying.	I know how you feel.
You'd say . . .	Show me.	Tell me.	Let me try!
You'd say . . .	Watch how I do it.	Let me explain.	You try it!
Pastimes?	Plays, films, television.	Music, conversations.	Playing sports.
Shopping?	Look and imagine.	Discuss opinions.	Try it on to test it out.
Choosing a car!	Read reviews.	Discuss with friends.	Test-drive what you like.

GO SMART ... Learning Styles

1. On the line master distributed by your teacher, make an X under visual, auditory, or kinesthetic. At the end add up your totals. What have you learned about yourself?

2. Look at the career choices below. Decide which learning style would be best suited to these careers. On the line master distributed by your teacher, put a **V** (visual), **A** (auditory), or **K** (kinesthetic) beside the career.

   Discuss in a group why you chose your answers.

actor	disc jockey	musician
architect	doctor	sales clerk
athlete	engineer	sound technician
construction worker	life insurance salesperson	zookeeper

3. Research three possible career choices that would suit your learning style. Add these career choices to your notes about your preferred learning style so that you can transfer these ideas to Tool 1: Personal Profile.

DO THE SEARCH

HAPPINESS ○ ○ ● ● ●
MONEY ○ ○ ● ● ●

REAL-TIME RESUMÉ

This job doesn't fit!

When he's not at school or at his part-time job, Theo plays guitar, writes songs, and listens to music as often as he can. He even uses his music equipment for his science and history tests by recording what he's supposed to study and then listening to it later. He remembers it better that way.

Theo works at one of the fast-food restaurants at the mall but he doesn't much like the job. The crowds don't bother him—in fact, he'd enjoy talking more to customers. However, there's little time to talk; he works in the back where all the food is prepared. Theo continues working to earn money, but the reality is: his part-time job is a big struggle.

YOU BE THE COACH

Why do you think Theo dislikes going to work? What do you think are Theo's top intelligences and preferred learning style? (See pages 23–25.) Make a list of five part-time jobs that you think Theo would enjoy. Now write a short rhyme or rap to explain to Theo why one or two of these jobs sound like a better fit for him.

REALITY CHECK

○ Part-time jobs, like full-time jobs, are more enjoyable when they involve your interests, preferences, and abilities.

○ Taking your intelligences and learning style into account when looking for part-time work means you'll not only develop necessary workplace skills, you'll also enjoy putting in the time.

○ Volunteering or co-op experiences (see pages 108–109) provide other opportunities to experience your strongest intelligences and learning style in action.

OUR HEROINE FEELS SHE'S WASTING HER TIME DOING ALL THESE CAREER INTEREST SURVEYS AND ASSESSMENTS IN CAREER STUDIES CLASS. MONIKA SAYS SHE DOESN'T NEED THEM BECAUSE HER CAREER DESTINATION IS CLEAR: SHE'S GOING TO BECOME A LAWYER JUST LIKE HER MOM WANTS...

Hey, girl, you've fallen into the "do-what-someone-else-wants-you-to-do" way of choosing a career!

WHERE ARE YOUR CAREER SURVEYS?

MR. LEWIN, THEY'RE A WASTE OF TIME. MY MOM WANTS ME TO BE A LAWYER AND I AGREE.

ARE YOU SURE?

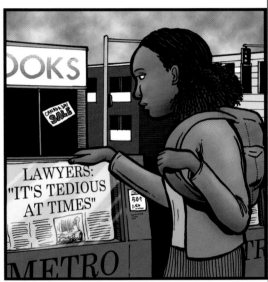

LAWYERS: "IT'S TEDIOUS AT TIMES"

YOU KNOW, MOM, EVERYONE NEEDS A PLAN B. MAYBE I WILL BE A LAWYER BUT I STILL NEED TO LOOK AT MY OPTIONS.

1. WHY SHOULD MONIKA CONSIDER OTHER OCCUPATIONS AS PART OF HER CAREER PLANNING?

2. IDENTIFY ONE OCCUPATION THAT IS YOUR FIRST CHOICE, OR "PLAN A," AND THREE OCCUPATIONS THAT COULD BE SECONDARY CHOICES — YOUR "PLAN B." NOTE THIS INFORMATION IN YOUR PORTFOLIO AND USE IT WHEN YOU ARE COMPLETING YOUR TOOLS.

What's Essential About Skills?

In the 1990s, a lot of research was being done to show that certain skills are critical to job success. Without these skills, your chances of succeeding in the world of work are dramatically lowered. The Government of Canada contributed to this research by launching the Essential Skills Research Project (ESRP). Through this project, nine essential on-the-job skills were identified.

Use the mnemonic device of making a sentence using the first letter of each word to try and figure out the Nine Essential Skills.

WHEN DISCOVERY CALLS, READ NEW TYPES OF WORDS CAREFULLY

To check your answers, go to Chapter 11, page 139. The Nine Essential Skills are listed there, along with a description of each.

People skills, such as being good at teamwork, are an asset in most work environments.

GO SMART ... Skills and Values

1. Examine the following situations. Which of the essential skills is needed in each career?

   - Armando is a custom carpenter. He researches popular furniture styles by browsing antique markets and going online. He works largely by himself but always asks his wife and kids for their opinion about his latest handiwork.

   - Heather is the production manager for a company that makes cameras. She answers questions for the sales representatives and travels across Canada and the United States. She uses her BlackBerry daily; it keeps her connected. She writes monthly reports.

   - Sam makes cheese. He creates new cheese products that he ships to clients all over Canada and the United States. He works closely with an accountant, his brother Raphael, to make sure all the books and accounts are up to date. He has been reading nutrition research to keep his products inventive and competitive.

   - Shoko is an entrepreneur in exotic fruit juices. She does the books, researches her competition, uses her computer daily to improve her product, and shares ideas with her partner, Adele, her best friend. Shoko and Adele are both taking a nutrition course at college.

   - You are a high school student. You work on projects and share ideas with classmates. You spend time reading and researching in the library and at home. You plan to begin an apprenticeship program after Grade 11. You do most of your work on the computer; you're thinking about spending more time on your geometry homework as a possible second area of study—most apprenticeships need it.

2. Now go over the five scenarios and write down two more values (defined in this chapter on page 24) that each of these people brings to his or her current career choices. Discuss your ideas with a small group of classmates. One example for each scenario is completed for you below:

   Armando: Knowledge

   Heather: Helping others

   Sam and Raphael: Success

   Shoko and Adele: Friendship

   You: Exploring

Read the Summary on page 31. Are there any ideas you are unsure of? Are there any skills you need to practise? If so, go back and review them.

Moving Forward

Remember the symbol that you created on page 23? It is your way to move forward in understanding yourself and your unique career adventure. At this point, add your visual symbol to Tool 1: Personal Profile.

In the coming chapters, you will have the opportunity to explore some opportunities for learning and working after high school.

Good luck on the next part of your journey!

A student might choose a spiral galaxy as her visual to represent her career path because it shows movement and complexity, and she might pursue a career in science.

This chapter introduced you to the following ideas:

1. Choose a career that you would like, not one that you think is a "good career." But remember to have a Plan B in case your Plan A career does not work out.

2. Embrace change. Change is opportunity. Your attitude will help you deal with changes that are out of your control.

3. Don't be afraid to make mistakes. Choosing a career path requires trial and error. Money should not be your only objective. A well-balanced life is far more rewarding.

4. Remember what you dreamed of being as a child? Following up on an early but lingering dream career might not be a bad idea.

5. Take into account your interests, abilities, skills, personality, influences, values, pastimes, challenges, and aspirations when considering what might be the best job for you.

6. There are at least nine ways of categorizing types of intelligence. Which types of intelligence are strongest in you? How might these intelligences lead to a career?

7. In the 21st century, the more skills you have, the better. A number of countries decided on nine essential job skills. The nine essential skills are listed on page 139. Which of these skills do you already have and which ones should you perhaps improve on?

Confident that you are ready to move forward?
Then go to the next chapter.

31

Putting It All Together

Who's the Boss of You?

- Who makes your decisions for *you*?
- What does it mean to "follow blindly"?
- How can you make sure that you consider the advice of others but also make choices that fit who you are and what you want to become?
- From this moment on, how can you start to be the boss of you?

Tool 1 still handy? In this chapter, add information about your approach to organization, time management, problem solving, and decision making.

3

How Well Do You Manage Yourself?

Personal management skills are valuable in your school life and in your home life. They include such skills as organization, time management, problem solving, and decision making. The stronger your personal management skills, the greater the control you have over your own life—and the more others will see you as responsible.

personal management
organizing, directing, and controlling yourself and your own behaviour

CHANGE YOUR HABITS AND YOUR LIFE WILL FOLLOW

Have you ever changed a **habit**? It's tough at first, but gradually your brain learns the new drill. The point is, personal management skills and habits can be learned. These skills and habits are just as valuable in the world of work as they are at home and at school.

Just because you feel you've come this far without using these skills consistently doesn't mean you can't develop them now: you can! But it will take some effort to change bad habits and replace them with good ones.

habit
something you have gotten used to doing without thinking

The Top 10 Reasons Employees Are Fired

1. Bringing their personal life to work with them.
2. Forgetting about teamwork and only looking out for their own best interests.
3. Arriving late and leaving early.
4. Sleeping at their desk on a daily basis.
5. Taking extra long lunch breaks each day.
6. Downloading anything and everything from the Internet.
7. Complaining about the job to anyone willing to listen.
8. Constantly searching for other jobs during work hours.
9. Lying on their job application or resumé.
10. Drinking alcoholic beverages on the job.

It takes real work to change a habit. Brain research tells us that you need to stop the bad habit for about 30 days before it starts to feel comfortable.

Keep matching up Tool 1 with the information found with Tool 2. If anything clicks for you, be sure to note it.

1. THINK OF THREE WAYS TO STAY ORGANIZED THAT COULD BE BENEFICIAL TO YOU.

2. A) SELECT AN UPCOMING TASK FOR WHICH YOU MUST STAY ORGANIZED. DESIGN A PLAN TO STAY ORGANIZED FOR THIS TASK AND FOLLOW THROUGH WITH IT.

   B) AT THE END OF THE TASK, NOTE HOW STAYING ORGANIZED HELPED YOU COMPLETE THE TASK.

GO SMART ... Self-Management on the Job

Here are some ways that good employees demonstrate self-management skills. What would each of these look like in the life of a typical high school student?

- Joshua arrives at work early every day to check his email and prepare for the morning meeting.

- You will never catch Elise without her Palm Pilot. It buzzes to remind her of meetings and appointments. She even uses it to schedule her yoga classes.

- Rick's job as an architect is very demanding. He works on large, complex projects, with tight deadlines. He keeps this stressful job under control by breaking each project down into manageable steps and assigning each step a deadline so that the whole project is always finished on time.

- Working as a mechanic at the busiest garage in the city is just the challenge Jin enjoys. She makes sure that she has her tools organized in separate compartments so that she can find them quickly whenever she needs them.

SELF-MANAGEMENT TODAY

1. In a small group, brainstorm ideas in response to the following. Remember the brainstorming rules: involve everyone; quantity over quality; think outside the box; don't judge; record all ideas. Use the line master distributed by your teacher.

   - What do you need to change to make it easier for you to attend every class, on time?
   - How can you make it more fun to use your agenda to organize your time?
   - How can you break down these kinds of assignments into manageable chunks:
     - reading a novel for English?
     - writing a lab for science?
     - preparing a presentation for history?
     - studying for a math test?
   - How can you get help when you need it?
   - What could you do to keep your notes more organized? Your workspace?
   - How can you make sure that you always have the materials you need for each class?

2. Look over your group's ideas. Think about the changes you need to make so that you have stronger self-management skills. Using some of the ideas from your group's brainstorming and any new ideas of your own, complete some reminders to yourself for each change you need to make.

Open that agenda and USE it!

What and Who Influences Your Future?

When you were younger, other people made all your decisions for you—parents, guardians, relatives, teachers. As you get older, you start to make decisions for yourself. One way to improve your decision making is to be aware of messages that influence your decisions.

You make choices all day, every day. You choose when to get out of bed, what to have for breakfast, whether or not to attend classes, and how much homework to complete. Every time you are faced with a choice, different messages pull you in different directions. Some of these messages come from external sources. Some come from inside yourself.

The more aware you are of the messages that might influence your decisions, the less likely you are to blindly follow one of them, without thinking about it. The more aware you are of these messages, the closer you come to making real decisions of your own.

STUDENTS INTERESTED IN SKILLED TRADES CAN ATTEND THE LUNCHTIME APPRENTICESHIP WORKSHOP ...

MELISSA'S ROCKET PROJECT DEMONSTRATED GOOD UNDERSTANDING OF THE CONCEPTS ...

I'M TERRIBLE AT MATH!

BALANCING WORK AND HOME MEANS WOMEN'S LIVES ARE MORE STRESSFUL

WOW, A WOMAN ELECTRICIAN. I'VE NEVER SEEN A WOMAN DO THAT BEFORE.

HEY, LET'S BOTH TAKE FOOD AND NUTRITION SO WE CAN BE IN THE SAME CLASS!

SCIENCE IS LAME. LET'S GO TO THE MALL.

THIS IS MY FAVOURITE CLASS. I LIKE MAKING STUFF THAT ACTUALLY WORKS.

WHY DON'T YOU GO INTO COMPUTERS?

WALK MY BROTHER HOME, START MAKING DINNER ... WORK STARTS AT 7:00 ... WHEN AM I GOING TO GET THAT ESSAY DONE?

IT IS A GOOD MARK BUT IT'D BE HIGHER IF YOU STUDIED.

INTRODUCTION TO TECHNOLOGY 83%

GO SMART ... Interpreting Messages

1. Read Melissa's messages.

2. With a partner, record your answers on the line master distributed by your teacher. Here's an example completed for you:

What's the message?	I'm terrible at math!
What's the source?	Melissa
Internal or external?	internal
+ or – ?	–
Possible response	You can't be good at everything, and you're great at lots of other subjects.

a) Identify a possible source for each of these messages.

b) Decide whether you think each one is an internal or external influence.

3. Imagine that Melissa is making a decision that will affect her future.

a) What decision do you think she is contemplating? How might each message influence her decision?

b) How can people respond to messages so that the message does not completely control their decision?

4. On your own, complete a second line master distributed by your teacher, starting with the following steps.

a) Consider the sources you listed in the first line master.

b) When you think about your future, from which of these same sources do you receive messages?

c) What are some other sources of influence for you?

d) Complete the rest of the table.

CHEMISTRY ⚪●●●●
DRAMA ⚪⚪⚪⚪●

REAL-TIME RESUMÉ

But I don't WANT to be a doctor

Once again, it was course selection time at Bayberry Secondary School. Ahmed had read the course selection material at least six times. He'd met with his guidance counsellor. He'd talked with his teacher. And he'd gone back to poring over the course offerings, more confused than ever.

"I just don't know what to do," Ahmed said to Julie over lunch in the local food court.

"Just pick—what's the big deal?" said Julie, munching on her fries.

"It's not that easy," Ahmed sighed, "My parents think I'm going to be a pharmacist or a doctor or something, but I'm getting 58 in chemistry this semester. Being in that Myth Busters skit is the closest I've ever come to doing well in science."

"Well, drama is your favourite subject. That should tell you something."

"Yeah, but they think it's a waste of time."

YOU BE THE COACH

How can Ahmed tell his parents that the career path they have chosen for him is not a good fit? Consider the tips below to give Ahmed your best reality check. Write your reality check in the form of a letter from Ahmed to his parents.

REALITY CHECK

- Parents or guardians are human and they make mistakes.
- Parents or guardians usually give advice that they think will guide their children toward a happy life in the future.
- No one knows you better than you, so you are the only one who can choose a career path that fits you best.
- Using an "I-message" is often the best way to express your thoughts and feelings, respectfully, in difficult situations. See the I-Message Formula on page 57 of Chapter 4.

Using Decision-Making Skills

Now that you are more conscious of the kinds of internal and external influences that can pull you in different directions, you are ready to learn how to make your own decisions. Making confident decisions does not happen by accident. Sometimes the consequences of hastily made decisions turn out to be good ones. But just as often, those consequences can be bad. If you are trying to decide which gum to buy, making a poor decision is not a big deal. If you are trying to decide which job to take, though, a poor decision could change your life.

However, all decisions have something in common—the process good decision-makers use to get the best possible results. So, how important is it to choose the right path for yourself after high school—one that "fits" who you are? Read on.

DECISIONS, DECISIONS: SHOPPING FOR JEANS

"I don't even know where to start," said Toni as she and Sarah entered the jeans store on Saturday morning.

"We're just buying jeans for school," Sarah reminded her. "It's no big deal."

"Really? Have you seen that wall full of jeans? I see at least six brands and 15 different styles. No big deal, eh?"

"OK, let's use our heads a little," said Sarah. "First of all, I'm not shopping for any old-lady jeans, so forget those two brands over there."

"And I only have $100 in the bank and I'm not spending it all on one pair of jeans," Toni added.

"I look best in boot-cut," Sarah continued, moving toward the boot-cut styles with new enthusiasm.

"And I definitely want dark wash—and not too much junk on the pockets," Toni added.

Sarah and Toni entered the change room area, each with an armload of jeans. "Good luck!" they called to one other. Soon Sarah was checking out her jeans in the mirror, while Toni poked her head out from behind the change room door. "There's no way I'm coming out in these. They should fit—but they don't even come down to my ankles. I'd look just great wearing *these* to school."

"Well, maybe you've got the wrong size," said Sarah, laughing along. "I'm happy with these, though. They're a good fit."

"Actually, you guys were in the petites section," interjected a salesperson. "That's why the jeans look good on you but not on your friend. But she'll probably find something just right two aisles over."

"No thanks!" groaned Toni. "That's enough trauma for one day. I'll come back next weekend, but please direct me to the right section!"

GO SMART ... Decision Making with a Partner

1. Read the Shopping for Jeans story on page 39 carefully.

2. Using the line master distributed by your teacher, think of the steps the two friends take as they go through their decision-making process. The first step is completed for you. Read it over carefully. You will have to complete the centre and right-hand columns for the other steps.

Jean Scenes	Decision-Making Step	When It's a Career Decision
"We're just buying jeans…"	Identify the decision you need to make.	What should I do after high school?

3. Have a look at the steps in the left-hand column on your line master. Make adjustments where you think they are necessary.

4. Now, work with your partner to complete the centre and right-hand columns. Consider each "Decision-Making Step" in the centre column. What would each of these decision-making steps look like when you are trying to make a career decision? Use the first completed step as an example.

5. In the story, what does Toni learn about getting help?

DO THE SEARCH ▶
6. How can you get help from an expert when you are making career decisions?

Using Research Skills

One of the most important skills you use in making good decisions is the skill of researching. The best researchers are good detectives.

When a detective is solving a crime, he or she must

- sort through information from witnesses, physical evidence, expert reports, interviews, and documents
- decide which information is connected to the crime and which information she can ignore
- understand which sources of information are trustworthy and which are not

DO THE SEARCH ▶
- know how to present the information so that it proves who committed the crime
- finish her investigation before the perpetrator is out of reach
- get help from other detectives, police officers, lawyers, laboratory technicians, pathologists, and others.

"Look Constable, the final piece of our jigsaw."

Ready to solve the puzzle?

USING GUIDING QUESTIONS IN RESEARCH

When you need to find information, you use a similar process—guided by the same kinds of questions used by detectives to uncover information.

Guiding Questions Chart

What do I need to know?	... so I can plan and problem-solve
• Where can I find the best sources for this information? (print, electronic, people)	• ... so I can avoid less trustworthy sources?
• How do I find what I need to know?	• ... and ignore what I DON'T need to know?
• Why do I want this information?	• ... because that will determine how I record it and organize it.
• When do I need to be finished this research?	• ... so I can plan out my time in advance.
• Who can help me when I need it?	• ... because I'll probably need some help.

GO SMART ... What Do I Need to Graduate from High School?

DO THE SEARCH

In a small group, use the guiding questions as well as the resources appropriate to your high school. Play detective and research the following:

1. What are the requirements to earn an Ontario Secondary School Diploma?

2. Which requirements have you already completed?

3. Which do you still need to complete?

4. In Grades 9 and 10, you must choose the right course type for you in all of your core courses (math, science, English, geography, and history). What are the different core course types to choose from?

5. What are the different core course types to choose from in Grades 11 and 12?

6. How can you decide which type is best for you in each subject?

7. Describe some of the alternative ways that you can earn credits (other than regular day-school courses).

8. Describe the kinds of support available in your school for achieving the literacy requirement.

9. How can you find a volunteer placement to complete your community involvement requirement?

What's Next?

In the coming chapters, you will have the opportunity to use your research and decision-making skills to

- explore *all* of the possible opportunities available for learning and working after high school
- examine each of these opportunities to determine which ones might be a good fit for you
- narrow down your range of options so that you can choose wisely.

Once you have made some "for now" decisions, you can start to plan a path from where you are now to where you eventually want to be.

Good luck on the next part of your journey!

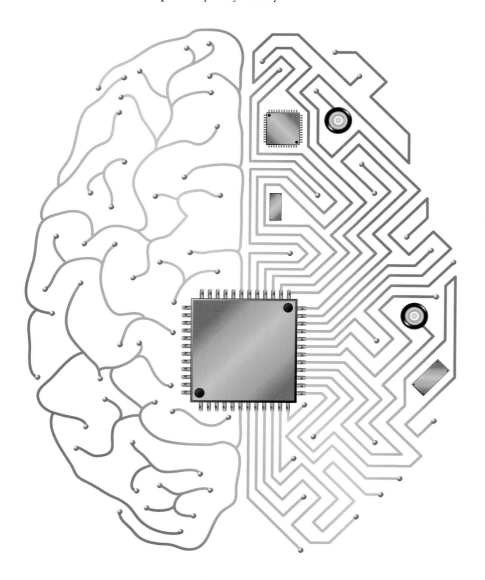

Read the Summary on page 43. Are there any ideas you are unsure of? Are there any skills you need to practise? If so, go back and review them.

This chapter introduced you to the following ideas:

1. You are in charge of your own life and your own choices.

2. Personal management is all about organization, time management, problem solving, and decision making.

3. Acting like an adult and behaving responsibly (for example, keeping your things in order, trying to do well at school) will encourage people to treat you like an adult.

4. Self-management is a useful skill. Qualities such as punctuality, preparedness, and organization, and skills such as organizing projects into manageable tasks and prioritizing, are all highly valued in the workplace.

5. Many different external and internal messages influence your actions and choices every day.

6. Though you may be influenced by many messages, ultimately, you are the boss of you—of what you will do in the future, and how you will do it. Knowing yourself is key to making successful career choices.

7. Making important life choices such as what job to pursue is never easy. Become a career detective, and get all of the information you need, starting with graduation requirements (page 41).

Confident that you are ready to move forward?
Then go to the first adventure.

43

PART 2

CHOOSE YOUR ADVENTURE

In this part of *Work Smart*, you will have the opportunity to

- size up and compare your post-secondary options in detail
- get to know the variety of learning opportunities for high school students
- identify different work opportunities using different sources such as the Internet, newspapers, and people you know
- research the education, training, and skill requirements of specific occupations
- compare open and hidden job markets
- identify specific trends affecting the world of work and self-employment
- learn about workplace safety issues
- identify the barriers that could interfere with your career plans
- communicate effectively with others in group work, interviews, and role plays using I-messages, reflective listening, and other strategies
- use teamwork to complete a variety of tasks

4 The Adventure: Straight to Work

The World of Work

"I really do see myself still putting out albums when I'm 70 years old, in all different genres."
—Nelly Furtado, award-winning singer-songwriter

Music has been a great career fit for Nelly Furtado, who says she comes from a musical family and tried to write her first song before she could read or write.

No matter what you do immediately after high school, your journey will eventually lead you to the world of work—a world of endless possibilities. Whatever you choose to do for a living, you will spend the vast majority of your day doing it. In fact, you will spend more time at work than you spend with your friends and family—more time than you spend doing anything else.

Your first work experiences could take any number of forms. Maybe you will work part-time while you complete high school or your post-secondary education. Maybe you will be a co-operative education student or an Ontario Youth Apprenticeship Program (OYAP) student. Perhaps you will work full-time—either to transition between other post-secondary options or because you've found the job you love and you intend to stay there.

Whichever way you choose to enter the world of work, you are in for an exciting adventure as you:

- look for a job that's right for you
- experience different work-style alternatives
- learn to survive and thrive in the world of work.

- What about you? What would you be willing to spend so much time doing?
- When people choose careers that fit them, what do they get out of it?

Remember to keep Tool 1 and Tool 2 handy. Watch for passions, preferences, and smarts that also describe you.

Top Reasons to Choose Work After High School

- You want to use your smarts to earn real money in a real job.
- You started to work part-time in a job you enjoy.
- You like the idea of learning on the job.
- You prefer learning by doing rather than learning by reading or listening.
- Research has led you to a "best fit" occupation that requires a secondary school diploma for an entry-level position.
- You want to be able to live independently soon.
- You made a connection with a great employer through co-op, OYAP, part-time, or volunteer work.
- You like the idea of "working your way up" in an organization.
- You found a career college or other vocational training program that will qualify you for a good job, help you earn higher wages, or earn a promotion.

Wise Words

"No bees, no honey; no work, no money."

—Proverb

DO THE SEARCH

Many people find the world of work is the best fit for them after high school.

GO SMART ... Work-Experience Scavenger Hunt

As a group, portion out the following list of scavenger hunt items equally among the group members. Be prepared to follow your teacher's time restrictions.

1. Find someone who …
   - went directly to work after high school
   - learned something new at work in the last 24 hours
   - got job-related training in the past year
   - was hired in the past year
   - ever got a job by answering a newspaper or online ad
   - has ever been injured on the job
   - has more than one paid job
   - works part-time
   - used a resumé in the past few years
   - participated in a job interview in the past few years
   - learned something important about their career from co-op, volunteer, part-time, or summer work while they were in high school
   - ever had a job where they worked from their home
   - ever got a job by accessing their network of friends or relatives
   - was fired from a job
   - was promoted recently
   - worked his or her way up in an organization
   - works "flex" hours.

2. Now find some adults in your school who have had these experiences on their career/life journey.
3. Collect a couple of details and a signature from each person.
4. Use the line master distributed by your teacher to collect your information. It looks like the table below.
5. When you return from the hunt, compare your collection to those of other groups.
   - Which group has the most interesting information to share?
   - Which group found the most surprising item?
   - Which group was able to find every item on the list?
   - Which was the most difficult item to find?
   - How many different people said "yes" to each of the items?

Scavenger Hunt Table

World of Work	Experience	Details	Signatures
1.			
2.			

If this career adventure suits you, add that information to Tool 3. Review Tool 3 regularly and move the options that best fit you into the inner circle.

Getting There: Open and Hidden Job Markets

Look back at your class's scavenger hunt results (page 47):

- How many people ever got a job by answering an online or newspaper ad?
- How many people ever got a job by accessing their network of friends and relatives?

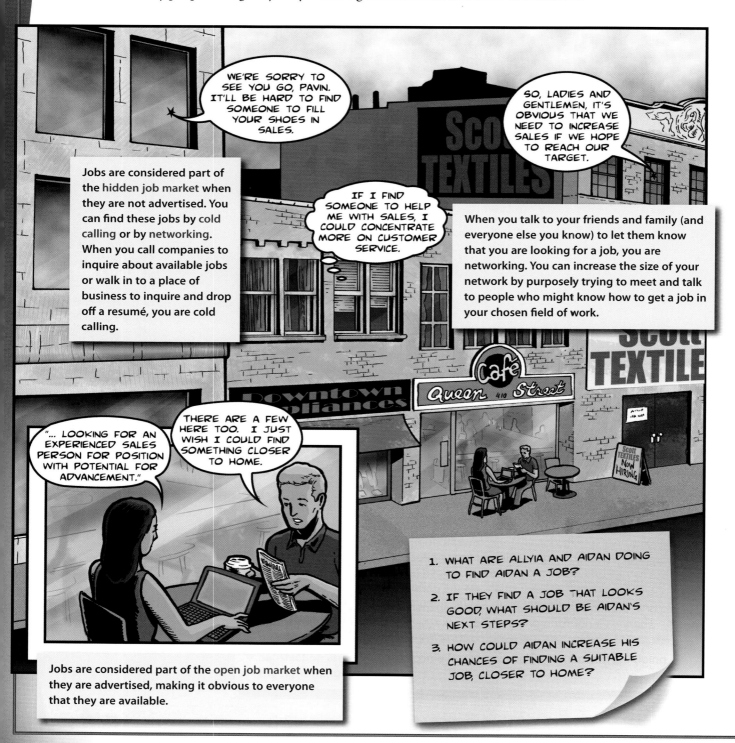

1. THE FAMOUS INVENTOR THOMAS EDISON ONCE SAID, "GOOD FORTUNE IS WHAT HAPPENS WHEN OPPORTUNITY MEETS WITH PLANNING."

   A) IDENTIFY THE STEPS AIDAN USED TO PLAN AN OPPORTUNITY FOR HIMSELF.

   B) HOW DID AIDAN MAKE HIS OWN LUCK?

2. A) THINK OF A TIME WHEN YOU DID SOMETHING THAT TURNED OUT REALLY WELL AND YOU "MADE YOUR OWN LUCK." WHAT STEPS DID YOU TAKE TO MAKE IT TURN OUT SO POSITIVELY?

GO SMART ... Growing Your Network

Using the line master distributed by your teacher (How Does a Network Grow?), print your name and a field of work you have already identified.

1. Post your completed line master in the space designated by your teacher.

2. Examine the sheets posted by your classmates.

3. Now think of some people you know well who work in the fields identified by the other students (your contacts). Print the name and relation of each contact (for example, aunt, neighbour, friend) on the other student's sheet. Then print your name underneath so the student knows who contributed each contact.

4. When everyone in the class has had a chance to contribute to the networking sheets, go back to look at your own sheet:

   a) How many contacts are possible just through this one class?

   b) In what other ways could you grow your network?

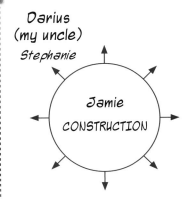

Darius (my uncle)
Stephanie
Jamie
CONSTRUCTION

Networking helps you to find the right job for you.

The Job of Finding a Job

DO THE SEARCH

If you want to increase your chances of finding the right job for you, then you will want to be aware of all of the jobs available in both the open and the hidden job markets.

Find a Job in the *Open* Job Market

Online job sites often provide tips on all kinds of job-search skills, e.g., writing a resumé, and FAQs (frequently asked questions) for job seekers.

- Do a web search for "**job sites**."
  - Use keywords to find job ads.

- Do a web search for Service Canada.
  - Search its job bank.
  - Find the location of your local Service Canada Centre.

Service Canada's job bank provides ads for entry-level and other jobs.

Service Canada is a government agency with local offices where you can get help finding a job, writing a resumé, and getting your Social Insurance Number (SIN).

- Visit your local **Service Canada Centre**.
  - Use its job bank.
  - Apply for your Social Insurance Number (SIN).
  - Participate in job-finding programs, such as Job Connect.

Many of the ads on job sites and in newspapers are placed by recruiting companies.

- Look through local newspapers.
  - Look for ads in the Classifieds, Careers, or Employment sections.

- Watch for Help Wanted signs outside local businesses.

Job fairs may be advertised on radio, television, or in newspapers.

- Attend advertised **job fairs**.

Social Insurance Number
government-issued number identifying one who is allowed to work in Canada

recruiting companies
businesses that are paid by other companies to find them potential employees

job fairs
events where employers display available jobs, accept resumés, and interview on the spot

You need a 9-digit Social Insurance Number (SIN) to work in Canada.

Human Resources Development Canada — Développement des ressources humaines Canada

SOCIAL INSURANCE NUMBER — NUMÉRO D'ASSURANCE SOCIALE

123 456 789

JANE DOE

EXPIRES/EXPIRE LE: 200X/ XX / XX
Y/A   M   D/J

Special job-finding programs connect you with an employer and subsidize your wages while you are new to the job.

Find a Job in the *Hidden* Job Market

- Tell everyone you know that you are looking for a job.

- Attend events where you might meet people in your chosen field.

- Design **business cards** to promote your skills and give them out.

- Find a business directory at a local library or Service Canada Centre.
  - Look for contact information for businesses in your chosen field.

- Use an online or print telephone directory to get contact information.

- Send a cover letter and resumé to companies or organizations you have discovered.

- Cold-call by telephoning or visiting companies or organizations where you would like to work.

business cards
small cards with all of your contact information on them

Ivan Petrochenko
Future Pet Products Buyer
Current Pet Lover
555-123-4567

Experience: Pet store kennel maintenance, pet sitting
Outstanding qualities: Reliability, teamwork, communication

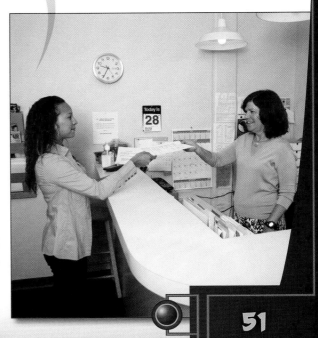

Cold calling is an essential skill for finding a good job.

GO SMART ... Finding a Job After High School

Find a partner who is interested in the same general field of work as you.

1. a) In the open job market, find as many job opportunities as you can (see page 50).

   b) Collect ads for all of the jobs that require a high school diploma or appear to require some high school education, but not a college diploma or a university degree. These are the straight-to-work ads.

   c) How many such ads did you find? Where was it easiest to find jobs for people going to work straight after high school?

   d) Highlight the kinds of training or experience they require.

   e) Highlight the kinds of skills and personal qualities they are looking for.

2. a) In the hidden job market, use an online or print telephone directory to find contact information for companies and organizations that appear connected to your chosen field of work.

   b) By telephoning some of these companies (see cold calling, page 51), find at least three that hire employees straight out of high school.

   c) List the contact information of these three employers.

3. a) Make a collage poster of your ads and the employer contact information you have found. Include a title on your poster that says Straight to Work and indicates the field of work they represent.

   b) Post your posters with all of the others in the classroom.

4. a) Review each poster of straight-to-work opportunities and read the highlighted sections of each ad.

   b) Which straight-to-work occupations appear to be the best fit for you?

   c) Record the names of at least three best-fit occupations on Tool 2.

WORK-STYLE ALTERNATIVES

temporary positions
jobs that are available for a limited time

freelance
selling your work to a company or organization for an agreed-on rate

contract position
employment with set terms (e.g., lasting several months or a year) and set objectives

flexible hours
work hours outside the typical 9–5 workday

Once you have chosen a field of work or an occupation that is right for you and once you have chosen a pathway to get there, your decision making is not over. You may get to choose *how* you will work, and this decision will affect which jobs you choose to apply for and which jobs you will accept.

It is not uncommon for people to have more than one part-time job, to work in **temporary positions**, to work **freelance**, or to work in **contract positions**. Some people enjoy the flexibility that these kinds of work-style alternatives provide. Others enjoy not only the flexibility, but the savings in costs and stress that they can get by working **flexible hours** or by working from home (see Chapter 5).

estion ut inibh eum elet.

A full-time job is generally considered to be approximately 35-40 hours per week or more. In a part-time position, an employee may work as few as 3 or as many as 30 hours per week.

Temporary positions can be full-time or part-time, but are intended to last for a limited time period because you would be replacing a permanent worker who is off temporarily or because the company's workload will increase temporarily (for example, maternity leave replacements, or holiday-time business increases).

Sectetue v wissi te mi ent atum inci blan vel ulpu net, deliquis ros- laore tie nis raesed iore Landre ptat dunt v gait henia rent exere nim vole utat dips ver Ect no- fa in- a rate

gait iam em

tionullam zzrit luptatu erciduisl utpatum dolestrud magnim nim ex eu faccum estion ut inibh eum elet.

Employees who work flexible hours may be able to choose the time they start and finish their day, avoiding rush hour, or making it easier to pick up children after school. Sometimes, employers and employees benefit financially by having the employee work at home. The employer saves on costs associated with providing work space and the employee saves on travel and clothing costs.

Unt utpat. Endrera esequipit alit adionse nisisit alisi. Acipit lorem zzriuscin hesit wisi. Ming eugue dolor si et laor alipo

San vel veli alit. ulla et l con mol alis

Lestio ing e num lut nit exero dolor strud ciduis

im dolestrud magnim nim ex eu faccum cil estion ut inibh eum elet. et, os- iis ore tat ait

eugue dip eu reugueuc core magna adipit nullam zzrirr.

People who work on a contract basis or freelance are selling their services to a company. They work on a project or for a time defined by the contract they sign with the company. They are not regular employees of the company and usually do not receive benefits. They may hold contracts with several companies at one time.

nt Ugait non ea commodo lorperit aut im praestrud te facip euissed eugait lu ud

Quamcons equat, consent lorperci eugait ad modigna autem vendreet dip

GO SMART ... Reflecting on Your Work Style

1. Remember the scavenger hunt you did on page 47? Who on your list has worked in an alternative work style (part-time, personal contract, freelance, temporary, at home)? What kinds of comments did they make about these different work styles?

2. Jot down some points in Tool 1: Personal Profile about the kind of work style that would be a good fit for you, if you had a choice. Remember that when you look for a job, you'll also want to consider the work-style alternatives available.

Staying Safe at Work

As a high school student, you probably feel that many rules in life simply get in your way. Think of some rules at home and school that get in your way. Now consider this question: Is it possible that some of these rules are intended to ensure your safety?

Safety in school is largely the responsibility of your principal and teachers. Your parents or guardians feel responsible for your safety at home. Many of the rules at work are also meant to keep people safe on the job. But sometimes, things can go wrong.

Imagine the story that goes with this picture.

- Every day, an average of 42 young Ontario workers are injured, made ill, or killed on the job.

- Young workers are injured more often by slips and falls than by any other workplace mishap.

- You have the right to know about any potential dangers in your job and how you can protect yourself.

- You have a right to refuse to do unsafe activities (jump to the section on Improving Communication on page 56 to find out how).

- Your supervisor has the responsibility to provide you with training and equipment to keep you safe.

- Most on-the-job injuries to young people happen in the service industry.

- If you are injured, in any way, you must report your injury to your supervisor.

Sandra fell off a ladder at work and broke her leg in several places. She was not able to return to work for months.

GO SMART ... Workplace Injuries

Prepare to play your role at a hearing that centres on proving who is responsible for this workplace injury. Conduct the hearing and see what happens! Your teacher will guide you with background information.

Life at Work

Whether your first job is a part-time job in a fast-food joint when you are 15 or a full-time job driving a truck, joining the world of work means change. Overnight, it seems, you move from the world of adolescents into the world of adults. It's a world with a whole new level of expectations and demands, rights, and responsibilities. However, you can make it in this world just fine—if you take what you learned in school and put it into practice.

CD's Story

CD working in sales at his dad's appliance store. A young salesperson with a sense of humour!

High school started well for CD, in Grade 9. In Grade 10, however, CD started to skip classes. By Grade 11, he'd missed so many classes that he was "kicked out for not attending" before second semester.

So he got a full-time job as a car jockey.

"I'm a big car guy," he says, "It was neat at the time. I got to drive cars all day. But it lost its appeal pretty quickly. Everyone there was unhappy. I didn't like having to report to people who treated me with no respect."

By the time August rolled around, CD decided to try a different high school. Unfortunately, CD—a self-described night-hawk—would sleep in until 2:00 in the afternoon, when the school day was nearly over.

CD was given a second chance with the STAR program, an alternative program offered by his school board. In the STAR program, CD didn't have to start class until 11:45 a.m. and he got to work more independently, at his own pace. CD caught up many of his missed credits, but was only allowed to participate in STAR for three semesters.

He returned to his local high school knowing that regular classes wouldn't work for him, so he chose to take a full semester of co-operative education. In co-op, CD decided to work at his father's appliance store as a salesperson.

"I didn't get paid, but I liked it. I knew I'd rather work than go to school—I knew school was not a huge thing for me." CD enjoyed working so much that he decided to stick with it instead of returning to school to finish his last couple of credits for his high school diploma.

Today, CD is happy with his chosen profession. His dad has been in sales for a long time and CD really enjoys sales too. "Maybe I've got sales in my genes," he jokes. He knows there is a lot more to being a good salesperson than pushing people to buy products: "You have to make customers happy. I've got a lot of problem solving to do in this job."

CD likes the idea of contributing to the family business and he likes what the job does for him: "I'm goal-oriented, money-oriented. I like the idea of making money and having it go into my pocket."

Still, he had sobering advice for students in high school: "Stay in school. You can always fall back on something else [if you finish school]. I have nothing to fall back on."

Over to You

1. Recent changes in education law mean that students must now stay in school until they are 18 or graduate. What kinds of support are available in your school for students who are struggling with attendance or other challenges to staying in school? What kinds of alternative programs are available in your school board?

2. How does the co-operative education program work in your school? What kinds of work placements do students have an opportunity to explore through your school's program?

3. If CD had completed Tool 1: Personal Profile to discover his pattern of interests, values, skills, strengths, and personal characteristics, what do you predict he would have discovered about himself?

Wise Words

"Choose a job you love, and you will never have to work a day in your life."

—*Confucius, Chinese philosopher*

Improving Communication with I-Messages

Communication in the workplace involves the same two skills as it does at home and at school: listening (receiving a message) and speaking (sending a message). Your ability to use these communication skills well will benefit you most when you are faced with uncomfortable or stressful situations.

Tran, for example, just got his first job at a fast-food restaurant. On his second day, his supervisor asked him to get a ladder and change the menu above the counter from breakfast to lunch and dinner. One glance at the ladder told Tran it was unsafe, but he dragged it over to the counter anyway. Stepping onto the first rung, Tran felt quite nervous. Still, he kept going because he didn't want to appear "weak" or uncooperative.

Then he remembered STOP.

The STOP Solution

Stop

Think

Object

Politely

When faced with situations that make you uncomfortable, STOP what you are doing, THINK about the possible consequences if you continue, and OBJECT POLITELY by using a respectful I-message. (For more about I-messages, see page 57.)

So this is what Tran ended up saying: "Tony, when I try to use this ladder to change the sign, I feel really uncomfortable because it wobbles."

And this is how Tran's supervisor responded: "Really? I had no idea the ladder was wobbly. Thank you, Tran—I wish someone had told me before." He then turned to the assistant supervisor and said, "Run over to the hardware store and buy a sturdy ladder so that Tran, here, can change the sign."

I-MESSAGES (SENDING A MESSAGE)

Most of the time, when we are frustrated, angry, or afraid, we let our emotions take over. We express the way we are feeling using a you-message because we don't know any other way to get our point across. In this wobbly-ladder situation, someone using a you-message might say, "Are you nuts? I'm not using this ladder!"

The problem with a you-message is that it puts the responsibility for your feelings on the person you are speaking to. The person reacts the only way they know how, by defending themselves: "Oh yeah—well, you're fired!"

By using an I-message, you take responsibility for your own feelings. Instead of blaming the other person for the situation, you simply describe the situation and your own feelings. Doing so allows the person listening to come to their own conclusions and to decide how to make things right.

At first, using an I-message feels awkward and fake but it becomes more natural with practice.

The I-Message Formula

When _____ ,	Describe situation objectively (the way a "fly on the wall" would)
I feel _____	Use an "emotion" word
because _____ .	Describe the direct effect on you

GO SMART ... Using I-Messages

With a partner, complete the line master distributed by your teacher. First create a you-message to suit the challenge. Then change that you-message into an I-message. Use your imagination and refer to the section above for help. One example is completed for you.

Challenge Table

Challenge	You-Message	I-Message
Your boss keeps scheduling you for extra shifts, even though you have told her it interferes with your homework.	"No matter what I say, you keep giving me extra shifts. You don't care about any of us!"	"When you schedule me for extra shifts, I feel frustrated because I can't get my homework done so I have to stay up too late and I end up exhausted."

HAPPINESS ○ ● ● ● ●
MONEY ○ ● ● ● ●

REAL-TIME RESUMÉ

Hate my job—Now what?

When Sam's uncle offered him a job selling cars at his dealership, he thought he had it made. Sam would work on a commission basis, which meant he would make 25 percent of the profit for every car he sold. Sam's uncle told him he could easily make $30,000 in a year. And he got to drive a new demo car to work every day.

Almost two weeks had gone by before Sam sold one car. He had difficulty approaching customers and negotiating with them. He knew his uncle was disappointed in him but Sam didn't know what to tell him. And he was starting to dread going to work every day.

YOU BE THE COACH

How should Sam tell his uncle he hates his job? Once he does tell him, how can he make sure he doesn't make this kind of mistake again? Give Sam your best reality check using the tips below. Write your advice in the form of an email.

REALITY CHECK

- This is one of those difficult conversations that might be easier if Sam used I-messages.

- Go back to Chapter 3 to remind yourself of how to make good career decisions.

BEING A REFLECTIVE LISTENER

If you want to be a good listener, get ready to work. Good listening requires concentration and thought. It's not just about hearing the words someone is saying—it's about understanding the message they are trying to send. The best way to show that you have heard the message is to reflect it back to the speaker, as if you were a mirror reflecting an image.

GO SMART ... Reflective Listening

1. Pick a partner. Listen carefully as the person tells you about something he or she is looking forward to. Use eye contact, nodding, and phrases such as "uh-huh" and "yes" to indicate you are listening, BUT DO NOT speak in any other way for three minutes.

2. When three minutes are up, complete the following statement to reflect back the speaker's message:

   "One thing I heard that seems important to you is …"

   After you complete the statement, don't say anything else. What is the speaker's reaction?

3. Change places and try this process again.

   a) How does this kind of listening differ from what you usually experience with friends and family members?

   b) How does it feel to be listened to in this way?

   c) How might you be able to use reflective listening at work when:

   • your boss is giving you instructions?

   • a co-worker is showing you how to do part of your job?

   • a customer is unhappy with the service he or she has received?

Learning to be a good listener will serve you well in any future job.

IT'S ALL ABOUT TEAMWORK

No matter where you work, you are likely to work as part of a team at least some of the time. Teamwork skills do not come naturally, but can be developed if you know what they look like.

GO SMART ... The Human Knot

1. Form a group of eight students and stand in a circle. With your right hand, hold the hand of someone near you, but not right beside you. Do the same with your left hand.

   Without letting go, work as a team to untie your human knot. Then discuss the following:
   - What kinds of roles did people play in your group?
   - What kinds of behaviours made your task easier?
   - What kinds made it more difficult?
   - How did people in your team feel at the end of the task?
   - What might have made them feel different?
   - How could you improve your teamwork the next time?

2. As a class, reflect on your group discussions and come to a consensus about what good teamwork looks like. Record and post your list of descriptors.

3. On your own, reflect and record the following information on the line master distributed by your teacher.

Good teamwork looks like . . .	An example of when I have shown good teamwork skills is when . . .	I can do better at teamwork by . . .
◦	◦	◦
◦	◦	◦
◦	◦	◦

Is Straight to Work for You?

Think about all of the students who started Grade 9 at your school last year. It might surprise you to know that around 50 percent of all students who start Grade 9 in Ontario choose work as their first option after high school.

Some people who choose to go straight to work after high school later choose to continue their education in college, university, or an apprenticeship program. Some earn certifications through vocational training programs that help them advance in their chosen occupation.

Anyone who really makes it in the world of work makes it because they know how to learn in the most important classroom of all—the workplace.

Read the Summary on page 61. Are there any ideas you are unsure of? Are there any skills you need to practise? If so, go back and review them.

 ... **Narrowing It Down**

Could straight to work be right for you?

 ◄ **DO THE SEARCH**

1. Do a web search for Career Cruising. In the Explore Careers sections, use the tools provided to find occupations that require a high school diploma, but not apprenticeship, college, or university.

2. Choose a few occupations to look at more closely.

3. For each of these occupations, review the information and interview sections. Review research skills in Chapter 3 if you need to.

4. Carefully read on and in between the lines to discover what kind of person would be best suited to these occupations (personality, learning style, values, etc.). Compare Tool 1: Personal Profile to these characteristics. Would any of these occupations be a good fit for you?

This chapter introduced you to the following ideas:

1. Many students (up to 50 percent) choose to go straight to work right out of high school. If you are someone who prefers to learn on the job rather than in school, this might be a good choice for you.

2. There are two job markets to be aware of when looking for work: the open job market (jobs that are advertised) and the hidden job market (jobs that are not advertised). Networking with friends and family helps to tap into the hidden job market.

3. Some tools for finding a good job after high school include: producing a business card, knowing where to look for potential jobs, learning how to network, and not being afraid to cold-call businesses that interest you.

4. There are many options for different work styles, from part-time jobs to temporary full-time positions, freelance or contract work, flexible hours, working from home ... you will need to find the work style that best suits your needs and personality type.

5. Work safety is a huge issue for young people entering the workforce right out of high school. You need to know your rights and feel that you can communicate your concerns about possible health and safety risks on the job to your manager or supervisor.

6. Being able to communicate with adults at work is essential to succeeding in your first job after high school. STOP (Stop Think Object Politely) is an acronym used to encourage young people to stay safe at work.

7. There are some basic skills for success at work: being a good listener, having strong teamwork skills, being able to learn new skills from others on the job, and welcoming training opportunities.

Confident that you are ready to move forward?
Then go to the next adventure.

61

The Adventure: Self-Employment and Entrepreneurship

Laughing All the Way to the Bank

Who's laughing now?

Jamel hit on a brilliant idea. A few years back he noticed that his word-processing skills were getting pretty good. Soon he boasted an amazing speed of 82 words per minute, just from typing all those essays. So after graduation, Jamel decided to become a virtual office assistant as a way to pay for his college tuition. Eventually, he plans to go into the hospitality/hotel industry.

When Jamel's buddies heard about the idea they started calling him "Keyboard." Today, however, Jamel's definitely having the last laugh. He now earns almost twice as much money per hour as most teens, by typing and transcribing for small businesses. He has an inexpensive web page to advertise his competitive rates. He pays no shipping costs. He does all the work from his bedroom. His bank account is growing ... and his clients have all agreed to be references on his college application.

It couldn't be more of a win–win situation.

And that's because the key to self-employment and entrepreneurship is need. If you have a service or product that the public truly needs and will pay for—and if you have the temperament of an entrepreneur—your chances of succeeding in this growing area are probably high.

- What personal qualities and strengths do you think Jamel has?
- Why do you think his service is so popular?
- What can you do well right now that people could use as a service?
- Why would people need it and why would they want to pay for it?

Remember to keep Tool 1 and Tool 2 handy. Watch for passions, preferences, and smarts that also describe you.

Self–Employment and Entrepreneurship: What Are They?

Self-employment and entrepreneurship are two popular ways to launch a career in Ontario. The two terms are often used interchangeably, but they are different.

SELF–EMPLOYMENT

Self-employed people get paid for their work, but not by an employer. Instead, they contract with a business to provide a certain number of hours of work and are paid an hourly rate or a **flat fee**. Some self-employed individuals work on site—that is, at the business. Others work at home. Freelance work operates in much the same way, with a self-employed person charging an hourly rate for services rendered, often working for many different companies simultaneously.

Self–Employment

+1 Contract with a business (on an hourly rate or for a flat fee).
"Contact small businesses in the area to get contract work."

flat fee
set amount of money charged for services rendered

Entrepreneurship

OPEN for Business

+1 Start and manage a brand new business.
"Advertise! Advertise! Advertise!"

ENTREPRENEURSHIP

Entrepreneurship is similar to self-employment except that entrepreneurs start and manage brand new businesses. For example, Jamel could have decided to contact small businesses in his area about the availability of contract work. Instead, he decided to advertise his services as a new student venture.

GO SMART ... Self-Employment

1. Identify at least one person you know who is either self-employed or has a business. Ask that person to explain
   - why he or she is an entrepreneur or self-employed
   - what that person enjoys the most about this style of work and what is the most challenging.
2. Record the responses on an index chard or small piece of paper and post them on a communal bulletin board, "The Good (and the Not-So-Good) of Going Solo."

If this career adventure interests you, add that information to Tool 3. Review Tool 3 regularly and move the options that best fit you into the inner circle.

63

How Self–Employment and Entrepreneurship Got to Be Big, Big, Big

In the years following World War II (1939–1945), few people would have imagined how popular self-employment and entrepreneurship would eventually become. A number of factors combined to fuel this trend:

- Since the 1950s, the economies of industrialized nations shifted from primary-industry and manufacturing economies to service economies (see "Canada's Sector Shares of GDP" below). By 1961, more revenue was being produced by the service sector than all other industries combined. In the service sector, opportunities for self-employment and entrepreneurship abound. Services are all about meeting people's immediate needs, so they can be endlessly customized depending on what people want today.

- During the 1980s, companies in Canada and other countries discovered that it was cheaper to downsize staff and contract out work to individuals. These individuals became officially self-employed. In many instances, they received a good hourly pay but no benefits from the company.

The pace of 21st-century life has opened up opportunities for many entrepreneurs specializing in personal services such as dog walking, cat sitting, house cleaning, errand running, and meal preparation. Who might have performed these services before? How did social changes open up new needs?

GDP
gross domestic product; the value of domestically produced goods or services in one year

sector share
a sector is one part of the economy that produces revenue; a sector share of the GDP refers to how much money of the total GDP that sector makes

Canada's Sector Shares of GDP (percent)

	Agriculture	Other resources	Manufacturing	Construction and utilities	Services
1951	11.8	7.0	29.5	7.2	44.5
1961	4.3	6.2	24.1	10.3	55.1
1971	3.0	5.2	21.8	10.1	59.8
1981	3.0	8.4	18.5	10.9	59.3
1991	1.7	4.6	16.3	10.0	67.3
1997	1.5	5.4	18.9	8.8	65.3

- New trade agreements were signed in North America and Europe that gave businesses and workers more flexibility in hiring practices. Today, for example, the customer service representative for a Canadian company might be a worker based in Delhi, India. This practice is known as out-sourcing. In many instances, companies can purchase cheaper services if they go outside Canada.

- New communication and information technology allowed people to talk to each other and send each other information electronically. This meant that people no longer needed to travel to a client who lived thousands of kilometres away—they could do business together from the comfort of their home offices.

He works for Office Tiger in Chennai, India but he might be talking to you soon.

IMPACT OF SELF-EMPLOYMENT ON SOCIETY

These developments have coaxed more and more Canadians to try self-employment and even to start their own businesses. Self-employment at home is an option that is appealing to many parents because it reduces the time they spend away from their children and decreases childcare costs.

Self-employment also appeals to retirees launching a second career—for example, as a consultant or coach in their field of expertise. Self-employment has helped some Canadians participate in the workforce when they didn't think they could, and it has helped others work many more years than they expected to.

Working at home is an option appealing to many parents.

GO SMART ... Job Trends

1. What is a trend? Identify some trends that you are aware of.

2. a) Examine "Canada's Sector Shares of GDP" on page 64. In what year was the services sector share of the Canadian GDP *double* all the other sectors combined?

   b) Make a statement about the services sector in Canada using the word *trend*.

3. Outsourcing is a controversial business practice. Some people think that it is unfair to take jobs away from Canadians and give them to workers in other countries just to save money. Opponents of this position argue that outsourcing can bring down the price of goods and services.

   a) Collect at least two articles about outsourcing and bring them to class. In each article, identify at least one advantage and one

DO THE SEARCH
disadvantage of outsourcing. Your teacher will give you some leads. Research on the Internet to find articles about outsourcing.

   b) Phone a few customer help lines and determine where the representative is located. Decide if the person's location makes any difference to you as a customer.

   c) Take a stand: *If you were a business owner, would you outsource?* Write a one-paragraph Opinion-Editorial (Op-Ed) piece or record a one-minute YouTube video stating your viewpoint. Give at least two reasons for your opinion.

4. Identify two ways in which self-employment and entrepreneurship have changed society and family life.

Self-Employment 411

Examine the information about self-employment on this page. What surprises you? What intrigues you?

SELF-EMPLOYMENT IN CANADA

- Between 1989 and 1997, self-employment accounted for 79.4 percent of job growth in Canada.
- According to Statistics Canada, the number of self-employed workers in Canada is still rising each year by an average of 1.9 percent.

Home renovator: One of the Top 10.

Top 10 Self-Employment Opportunities in Canada
(based on potential for growth)

- Home renovator
- Pet-related products and services
- Catering
- Cleaning
- Wedding planner
- Dietary consultant
- In-home beauty services—e.g., hair styling
- Sewing and alterations services
- Services for seniors—e.g., injury prevention, home visits
- Life/business coach

WHAT CAN YOU EARN?

Hourly rates for self-employed individuals and entrepreneurs start at around $18/hour, although some labour that is unskilled and performed by someone under the age of 20 might fetch only $12–$15/hour. Highly skilled professionals can earn several hundred dollars an hour or even more.

In some cases, you might not charge an hourly rate. Instead, you would estimate how much the whole job is worth and quote a flat fee (see page 63). Flat fees are often used for individual projects, such as shovelling a driveway or typing a report.

The money you receive from your clients is called **gross pay**. As a self-employed person, you must pay all your expenses and reserve a portion of your earnings for income tax and Canadian Pension Plan contributions. Some self-employed workers must also charge GST (goods and services tax), which they then must pay back to the government. (See "Employee or Self-Employed?" on page 70.) If you **subcontracted** any work to other individuals, you would have to pay them as well. What is left over is called **net pay**.

gross pay
pay before expenses or taxes have been deducted

subcontracted
assigned to someone else to do

net pay
pay after expenses and taxes have been deducted

GO SMART ... Business Advice

1. Tina wants to start a business selling wooden CD stands but she has no idea what to charge. Should she use an hourly rate or a flat fee? She wants to make a nice profit and produce reasonably priced CD stands that people will want to buy. Help Tina figure out what she needs to do by

   DO THE SEARCH

   • advising her where to look for information

   • explaining which method of payment would be preferable and why

   DO THE SEARCH

   • outlining three examples of expenses she should consider

   • reminding her of the difference between gross and net pay.

   Present your information to Tina in a role play. You are the business advisor!

2. Identify one self-employment/entrepreneurship career area that appeals to you and research it in more detail. Start with the "Top 10 Self-Employment Opportunities in Canada" list from page 66. Then go to the CanadaBusiness website, which gives you almost 100 business ideas categorized according to type—trades, repair, arts-related, personal, and so on. Your teacher will provide you with the link. Once you find a specific business that appeals to you, research it in more detail using a search engine.

   Research to find more information about self-employment and home-based businesses in Canada.

3. How is this business opportunity stacking up against your passions, your preferences, and your smarts? Don't decide yet. This is just a check-in. You'll have a chance to make your final decision later.

PROFILE How a 15-year-old got 5 million visitors

Catherine, seen here with friend and business partner, Dave, is an example of a young entrepreneur harnessing the unlimited possibilities of Internet technology.

15-year-old Catherine Cook was flipping through a yearbook one day, noticing how *dead* it seemed. How much better, she thought, to have a yearbook that could travel with you throughout your life—one that would always have room for new pages and unlimited friends and autographs.

So Catherine, her friend Dave, and her brother Geoff decided to create a social networking site called myYearbook. Catherine jotted the name down in her notebook and added smiley faces to the two o's. And that was it. The website was born. Today it has 5 million members along with multiple streams of revenue from advertising and its own store. With a 5-million-member customer base, Catherine and her team definitely qualify as successful youth entrepreneurs.

Catherine was recently interviewed by RetireAt21. This is what she said:

What advice would you give someone who wants to make a social networking website?

I would tell them to stay true to a certain core group. Now that there are two giant mass market social networking sites, the easiest way to succeed is to offer users something more specific than "finding friends."

Is being an entrepreneur in your blood or can you learn it?

I think it is something that can be learned, but only if you have a suitable mentor that can give you advice and help you out once in awhile. I had my older brother, Geoff, to go to for business advice, and I know it would have been many, many times harder to raise the **venture capital** and deal with investors without his help and experience.

What is the best advice you have ever been given?

Probably to never give up. Sometimes it was really hard to keep up with the site along with my school work and other responsibilities, and just being told that somehow I'll get through all the work I have helps.

What advice would you give to a young entrepreneur setting up their first business?

To never be scared of asking for advice and to use all available resources to find their way. I think it's important to look for answers, and if you can't find them yourself, to get a friend to help you out.

Over to You

1. Summarize the two big ideas about entrepreneurship illustrated by Catherine's story.

2. Which part of her advice is most relevant to you? How could you use that advice today?

3. Catherine has agreed to take your questions by email for one afternoon. Write a business-like email to Catherine asking her one additional question you have about starting up a business.

   ○ Include a salutation and closing.

   ○ Add a few details about yourself.

   ○ Relate your question to yourself. Why are you asking it?

venture capital
money invested to grow or expand a business

Do You Have What It Takes to Work for Yourself?

Working for yourself sounds so great—the freedom, the flexibility, the competitive hourly wage. The problem is, that's only half the story.

Self-employed people have lots of responsibilities that employees don't have. By law, they must keep complete records of the way they do business. They have only themselves to depend on when times get tough. And they always have to think about marketing their services. Just check out Dan's day.

1 You have to market yourself! Otherwise, no one will know about you. How are you going to do that?

2 When the client calls, listen carefully to the description of the assignment or contract. Ask for a written follow-up. It can be as simple as an email.

3 Agree on an hourly rate.

 **6** Wait to get paid and start all over again!

4 Do the work, even if it's tough.

5 Invoice for services and file the paperwork.

Employee or Self-Employed?

Employees	The self-employed
• Receive a regular paycheque	• Invoice and collect payment for services rendered
• Get vacation and sick pay	• Pay for their own sick days and holidays
• Qualify for medical benefits	• Buy their own insurance
• Are guaranteed an acceptable work environment	• Pay income tax and Canada Pension Plan contributions out of their earnings
• Have income tax and Canadian Pension Plan deducted from their pay	• Collect GST and file a quarterly GST return
• Receive a statement of earnings at tax time	• Maintain basic bookkeeping and filing procedures
• Receive **severance pay** if applicable	• Find new clients when work runs out

severance pay
payment made to a terminated employee

Wise Words

"Nobody talks of entrepreneurship as survival, but that's exactly what it is and what nurtures creative thinking."

—Anita Roddick,
founder of The Body Shop

GO SMART ... Business Skills

1. What skills does Dan use to get business and keep it? What skills does he use when he is actually doing the work? Make a two-column list.
2. Would you like to work like Dan? Why or why not?

TAKE THE TEST

PERSONALITY PLUS

Being self-employed or an entrepreneur also takes a certain personality and mindset. It's hard to stay motivated when the boss is not around. Also, it can be a fairly lonely and unpredictable life. Some people like the security of a steady paycheque and the opportunities to socialize at the office. How about you? Do you think you have the personality to go solo? Take our test to find out.

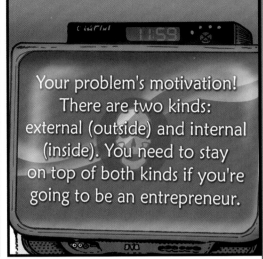

SOME BOSS OF ME I AM.

OUR HERO WANTS TO BE A YOUNG ENTREPRENEUR. KAY HAS A NICE PART-TIME LAWN BUSINESS FROM MAY TO OCTOBER. BUT SOMETIMES...HE JUST LOSES STEAM AND WONDERS IF HE ACTUALLY *NEEDS* A BOSS.

Your problem's motivation! There are two kinds: external (outside) and internal (inside). You need to stay on top of both kinds if you're going to be an entrepreneur.

IDENTIFY YOUR EXTERNAL MOTIVATORS FIRST. IN YOUR CASE, THAT'S COLD CASH. THEN THINK ABOUT HOW YOU MAKE YOURSELF FEEL. ARE YOU PROUD OF YOURSELF WHEN YOU GET THE JOB DONE? THAT'S YOUR INTERNAL MOTIVATOR.

OK, 3 LAWNS TODAY, 2 TOMORROW X $15, PLUS $25 FOR MR. DAVIS... FRONT-AND-BACK... HEY! NOT SO BAD!

To STAY MOTIVATED, I'LL THINK OF...
- WHAT I CAN EARN
- HOW IT LOOKS ON MY RESUME
- HOW DISAPPOINTING CLIENTS IS BAD FOR BUSINESS
- HOW IT MAKES ME FEEL —PROUD & ACCOMPLISHED.

1. THINK OF FOUR FACTORS THAT WHAT WOULD MOTIVATE YOU TO START YOUR OWN BUSINESS. WHICH OF THESE FACTORS ARE (A) INTERNAL AND (B) EXTERNAL MOTIVATORS?

2. WHAT BUSINESS DO YOU THINK WOULD BE A GOOD ONE FOR YOU TO LAUNCH IN THE SUMMER? EXPLAIN WHY THIS BUSINESS WOULD BE A GOOD FIT FOR YOU.

REAL-TIME RESUMÉ

Help, I can't say "No!"

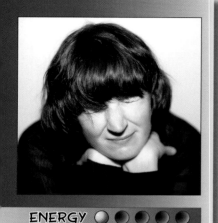

ENERGY ⬤⬤⬤⬤⬤

MONEY ⬤⬤⬤⬤⬤

Student entrepreneur Cara loves her part-time business. She runs errands for busy professionals who live in her apartment building on Friday night and on weekends. However, she has one client—Nancy—who is asking her to perform more and more services. Cara is squeezing in the extra work but she doesn't feel comfortable about it. Sometimes she is not paid for up to 45 minutes of her time. Occasionally, she runs late getting to other clients.

Cara doesn't want to offend Nancy but she doesn't know how to say "No."

Cara's business card says that she will do grocery shopping, pick up dry cleaning and mail, and water plants. She does not cook, pet-sit, or babysit. In her original interview, Cara talked about the services she offered and Nancy seemed satisfied. However, in recent weeks, Cara has been asked to put the groceries away, begin dinner, and feed Nancy's cats.

YOU BE THE COACH

If Cara tells Nancy that she can no longer perform these extra services, what do you think will happen? Give Cara your best reality check using the tips below. Write your advice in the form of an email. Then compare your reality check to the one provided by your teacher.

REALITY CHECK

- Contracts in writing signed by both parties protect against misunderstandings that occur down the road. A contract is any agreement that is signed and dated by both parties.

- Extra services can be billed at an extra charge on an invoice. However, it is usually better to talk about the overtime rate upfront.

- Saying "No" is not impolite—it simply means that you are setting boundaries. (For more about saying "No," see Chapter 11, page 142.)

Read the Summary on page 73. Are there any ideas you are unsure of? Are there any skills you need to practise? If so, go back and review them.

Calling All Ontario Student Entrepreneurs!

If entrepreneurship appeals to you, then guess what? Your government wants to help. Check out the assistance provided by the Government of Ontario:

- **The Secondary School Business Plan Competition** invites high school students to submit a business plan "from the highly technical to the creative arts and everything in between." The government wants something original. Before submitting the plan, students are asked to consult a business plan guide and discuss it with their teachers. They compete locally, and the winner of each competition becomes a regional finalist.

- **Non-profit organizations in Ontario** that support young entrepreneurs (12–29) through education, programs, and mentoring may receive $100,000 annually.

- **Summer Company** is an Ontario government-sponsored program designed to help young people aged 15–29 start up and run their own summer business. If you are selected, you could receive up to $3000 in funding.

DO THE SEARCH

This chapter introduced you to the following ideas:

1. Self-employment and entrepreneurship live where *need* meets *opportunity*.

2. Self-employed people may still work for others, by contract or on an hourly (freelance) basis. Entrepreneurs have their own business and work for themselves.

3. Self-employment and entrepreneurship expanded after the 1950s with a shift from manufacturing to service economies.

4. In the 1980s, companies realized it was cheaper to downsize and contract out work. New trade agreements gave businesses more flexibility, including outsourcing work to other countries.

5. Self-employment has changed the structure of society: parents stay at home to work with small children; people work after retirement; and society accepts more flexible work schedules.

6. Do you have the motivation and discipline to work for yourself? Can you manage the financial unpredictability and solitary work?

Confident that you are ready to move forward?
Then go to the next adventure.

73

The Adventure: Apprenticeship

Learning When You Were Little

Think back to when you were a little kid.
   Do you remember:

- building sandcastles on the beach?
- helping to make pizza with your favourite toppings?
- building houses, cars—maybe even whole cities—out of interlocking blocks?

Maybe you can still recall how focused you were as you placed each piece right where you wanted it—how exciting it was to watch your project grow. Do you remember the sense of contentment you felt when you had finished your creation? How proud you were to show your work to family and friends?

What would it be like to point to THIS

and say

or THIS

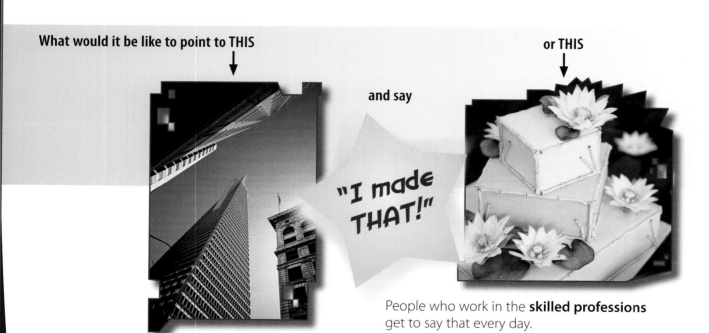

"I made THAT!"

People who work in the **skilled professions** get to say that every day.

skilled professions
occupations requiring expertise in using specific, hands-on skills and related knowledge, gained through an apprenticeship program

- Who helped *you* learn how to make things when you were little? An older family member? A friend? How did they help you learn?
- Did you enjoy this kind of learning? What did you do? Did you learn how to cook? How to fix things around the house? Build a birdhouse? Plant a garden?
- How do you think learning a skilled profession might be similar to the hands-on learning you have been doing your whole life?

 Remember to keep Tool 1 and Tool 2 handy. Watch for passions, preferences, and smarts that also describe you.

What Are the Skilled Professions?

Skilled professions are occupations that require you to be very good at using your hands, body, and mind to build, fix, or create. Because these occupations require a high level of hands-on skill development, you must complete your post-secondary education through an **apprenticeship program** if you intend to pursue a skilled profession.

The skilled professions can be divided into four main groups, called **sectors**.

apprenticeship program
post-secondary education required to become a skilled professional

sectors
categories of different kinds of work activity

Automotive and Motive Power
- Auto body repairer
- Motive power machinist
- Automotive service technician
- Motorcycle technician
- Small engine technician

Construction
- Brick and stone mason
- Plumber
- Carpenter
- Sheet metal worker
- Tile, terrazzo, and marble setter

Industrial
- Aircraft maintenance engineer
- Draftsperson, mechanical
- Industrial mechanic (millwright)
- Fitter welder
- Tool and die maker

Service
- Appliance service technician
- Arborist (tree specialist)
- Baker
- Early childhood educator
- Hairstylist

Only a few examples of skilled professions in each sector are shown here. Before you decide whether this is a good career path for you, be sure to become familiar with as many examples of skilled professions as possible.

DO THE SEARCH

GO SMART ... Jeopardy

1. In a small group, collect the background information needed for a Jeopardy game using the resources introduced by your teacher.

   a) Find the section that lists skilled professions (or apprenticeships) by sector.

   b) Choose several examples of professions to discover what these professions are about. Choose at least one occupation from each sector (for a total of four occupations).

   c) Find one detail in the description of each occupation that might stump others during a Jeopardy game. Turn each of those details into Jeopardy-style questions.

   d) For each of your choices, print the name of the occupation on one side of a recipe card and the matching question on the other.

   e) Combine your cards with those of other students in your class.

   f) Use the cards to run a Jeopardy-style game involving your whole class.

2. Think about the variety of skilled professions you have learned about, and choose a few that you find interesting enough to research further. Your teacher will provide you with a line master for this purpose.

   Return to the apprenticeship resources provided by your teacher, and reflect on the following:

   - What appeals to you, so far, about the skilled professions?

   - What parts of your personal profile make the skilled professions a good choice for you?

   - What parts of your personal profile make these professions a bad choice for you?

   Place your reflection in your portfolio.

If this career adventure interests you, add that information to Tool 3. Review Tool 3 regularly and move the options that best fit you into the inner circle.

75

Sandcastle building 101. You probably learned from the experts.

apprentice
someone learning a new trade or skill (from a journeyperson)

journeyperson
someone who is experienced and certified in a particular skilled profession

How Does Apprenticeship Work?

Remember those pizzas and sandcastles you learned to make as a kid? How do you think you learned those skills?

You probably didn't soak up the information while sitting at your desk or reading a book. Instead, you learned from an expert, someone who had knowledge and experience they could share with you. You learned by doing—by trying it out, asking questions, and listening while the expert (grandmother, father, brother, friend) explained how to avoid potential problems.

This is exactly how apprenticeship works. The **apprentice** (learner) learns from a **journeyperson** (expert) by doing the work involved in the skilled profession. A plumbing apprentice, for example, learns about plumbing by working with a certified plumber on the job. The same goes for a machinist, cook, or brake technician. The largest portion of learning in an apprenticeship program happens on the job.

Learning how to make a pizza.

Of course, you will still do some of your learning from a book. Every electrician needs to know about circuitry (physics) before wiring a house, and every hairstylist needs to know something about pH (chemistry) before colouring hair. The advantage of being an apprentice is that you get to apply that information to your work every day.

Wise Words

"When I began the Apprenticeship2000 program, I could never have imagined the doors that would open for me in the years following my graduation. In fact, I had no idea that training I was to receive during the program itself would be so rewarding."

—Sarah, Apprenticeship2000 Manufacturing Technology success story

Learning on the job!

GETTING STARTED IN AN APPRENTICESHIP PROGRAM

Unlike college and university, where getting started can be as simple as filling out an application form, getting started in an apprenticeship program is a little more complex. The first step in starting an apprenticeship program is finding an employer who will agree to hire you as an apprentice.

Tyler@notmail.com
<Tyler@notmail.com>

Tyler says
So how long does an apprenticeship program take?

Jay says
Just started today
Could be 2–5 years …
Depends which one you choose
Mostly it's learning at work
And you get paid

Tyler says
Mostly at work, eh?
How much in-school?

Jay says
I have to do 2 months in-school after I've worked for around 10 months.
Then back to work. Happens 3 times like that, then I should be done

Tyler says
How much does all that cost?

Jay says
The school part costs about $700 each time but that's books and everything and have you seen how much Janice is paying for college? It's way more, like almost $3000

Tyler says
I know

Jay says
And I'm getting paid the whole time too—15 bucks an hour—except when I'm in the school part

Tyler says
Sweet! Sign me up, man

Jay says
Uh … you need to graduate first
Why don't you go to guidance and sign up for co-op for next semester
You can join OYAP and start your apprenticeship that way—wish I'd done that

Tyler says
What about graduating?

Jay says
You can do everything at once that way—co-op, OYAP, credits
The guidance counsellor will explain it better

Tyler says
OK … g2g

> Apprenticeship programs are regulated by the Ontario Ministry of Training, Colleges and Universities (MTCU), just like college and university programs.

> One of the most challenging steps to becoming an apprentice is finding an employer (sponsor) to hire and train you.

> Training consultants from the MTCU meet with you and your sponsor, and provide you with details about what you must do to complete the program.

> The in-school portion takes place in an MTCU-approved training facility.

> Sometimes you have to write an exam to get your Certificate of Apprenticeship.

> You have to buy your own tools for some apprenticeship programs.

> You can get a special loan to buy tools, sort of like a student loan.

> You can find an MTCU training facility at a college or a private or union-owned training centre.

> When you are finished your program, you are a certified journeyperson with a Certificate of Apprenticeship.

PROFILE When the Light Went On

Andrew figuring out what he likes and what he is good at.

With only one more semester to complete his high school diploma, Andrew may not be able to foresee his future, but he sure knows what he would like his next steps to be.

In Grade 11 Andrew took a computer engineering course that literally turned on the lights for him: "We were doing stuff like building circuits to turn on lights bulbs, and it came easily." That's when he first thought that "electrician" might be the perfect career choice.

One day, Andrew's dad told him about a summer learning opportunity he'd heard of at work. "I thought it would be neat," says Andrew, "because it covered so many of the trades. I would get to see if I really liked electrical for my career."

So Andrew signed up for Introduction to the Technical Trades, a summer co-operative education opportunity run by Magna International's Technical Training Centre. Over a seven-and-a-half-week period, the course gave participants hands-on experience learning a different trade every week, including welding, millwright, lathe, PLC, robotics and pneumatics, and electrical.

For each of the different areas, students spent the first half a day or so learning theory and safety, but the rest was learning on the job. "Which was good," says Andrew. "I find hands-on a lot easier to learn than being told stuff."

Andrew especially liked the electrical course: "The guy teaching electrical was a highly certified guy. He had us building advanced circuits, and even though I was the youngest guy in my group, it seemed to come easily to me."

And he was pretty happy, too, about the bonuses he got for participating in the program: $8.00/hour and two high school co-op credits.

Andrew was recently accepted into two electrical engineering technology programs at Humber and Mohawk Colleges of Applied Arts and Technology. Getting sponsorship as an apprentice straight out of high school might be a little more complicated than following the college-first route, but Andrew hasn't given up on that pathway yet. He will continue looking for a sponsor until he starts a college program in the fall.

His advice to other high school students? "Choose something that's fun and comes easily to you. Don't go after something just because of what it's called or something. You want to really enjoy your job; otherwise, it will be a pretty miserable life."

GO SMART ... The Employer's Perspective

Imagine that you are an employer in a sector that interests you (motive power, construction, industrial, or service) and you are looking for a new employee. Answer the following questions:

1. What do you think are the pros and cons of hiring an apprentice instead of a journeyperson?
2. What kinds of experience, skills, and personal qualities would you hope to find in an apprentice?
3. What would a high school student need to do to get hired by you (as an employer)?
4. How could a high school student use their own network to find an employer?

1. THINK OF A PART-TIME JOB OR AN APPRENTICESHIP OPPORTUNITY THAT WOULD APPEAL TO YOU.

    A) DEVELOP A PLAN TO GET SOME EXPERIENCE IN THE AREA BEFORE APPLYING FOR THE JOB OR APPRENTICESHIP. WORK WITH A CLASSMATE AND SHARE IDEAS.

    B) IDENTIFY THREE PEOPLE YOU COULD APPROACH TO GET IDEAS ABOUT BEING HIRED FOR THIS KIND OF WORK OR GAINING EXPERIENCE IN THIS AREA.

DO THE SEARCH ▷

GO SMART ... Starting Out with College

Form a small group with some other students who are interested in the same sector of skilled professions as you are. Each member of the group should choose one skilled profession to investigate.

1. Using the line master provided by your teacher, do some research that would help you use the advice provided by the Career Coach on page 79.
2. Go to the website recommended by your teacher, or use the print resources provided by your school.
3. For this activity, focus on diploma programs (*not* apprenticeship programs) offered through Ontario colleges of applied arts and technology.
4. Find diploma programs in your chosen sector offered in three colleges, and complete the line master distributed by your teacher.

The Ontario Youth Apprenticeship Program (OYAP)

- For students enrolled in high school co-op who are interested in a specific skilled profession
- Your work in OYAP counts two ways:

| You earn high school credits to complete your diploma. | **+** | You earn credit toward the hours and skills needed to complete your apprenticeship program. | **➡** | You're on your way to an exciting new future as a skilled professional! |

Wise Words

"Participating in OYAP has put me closer to my dream of becoming a fully certified auto mechanic."

—*Jennifer, apprentice automotive service technician*

HOW DO APPRENTICESHIP AND THE SKILLED PROFESSIONS SUIT YOU?

Could an apprenticeship program leading to a skilled profession be right for you?

Top 10 Reasons for Choosing Apprenticeship After High School

1. You enjoy fixing, building, or creating.
2. You enjoy learning by doing more than learning by reading.
3. You like the idea of earning money while you learn the skills of your profession.
4. Your favourite courses in high school are technological or hospitality studies.
5. You like the idea of learning hands-on skills.
6. You enjoy learning math, science, and communication skills more when you know how you will use them in the real world.
7. You like seeing the product of your work.
8. You have at least one "best fit" occupation that requires completion of an apprenticeship program.
9. You have met someone in a skilled profession who has what seems to be the perfect job for you.
10. You want to own your own business one day.

Wise Words

"Things have changed … I was taken from school at once upon my father's death (in 1847) and placed in the office of the *Hannibal Courier* as printer's apprentice, and Mr. Ament, the editor and proprietor of the paper, allowed me … board and clothes but no money."

—*Mark Twain*

The Future of the Skilled Professions

In Canada, it is not uncommon for people to change occupations several times in their adult life. This should comfort those interested in the skilled professions: future job prospects in this area promise to be very solid for a long time to come.

In other words, if you invest your time and energy in an apprenticeship program now, you are likely to have job security well into the future.

Surveys of employers suggest that there is now—and is likely to be in the future—a shortage of journeypersons in Canada. A survey of small and medium-sized businesses conducted in 2000 showed that many businesses could not find suitable skilled professionals, leaving 1 in 20 jobs unfilled. In addition, many baby boomers who currently work in the skilled professions are expected to retire over the next few years, leaving even more positions waiting for the right people to fill them.

A survey conducted by the Automobile Parts Manufacturers Association suggests that a growing number of retirements over the next few years, or what is referred to as the "greying of the workforce," will result in a rapidly growing demand for skilled professionals and technicians.

Skilled tradespeople are retiring in large numbers with few qualified people to replace them.

Similar surveys of employers in the construction sector found similar results:

- Their workforce is aging.
- Many will be retiring soon.
- Fewer young people are entering their workforce.
- Younger workers are not completing their apprenticeship training.

Despite this evidence, it is difficult to determine whether the shortage of skilled professionals will be any greater than the predicted shortage of other kinds of workers in Canada. Anyone planning to enter the workforce is advised to investigate the job prospects for their chosen field before investing in post-secondary education.

—Adapted from *Solving the Skilled Trades Shortage*, Conference Board of Canada, 2002.

GO SMART ... Skilled Professions

DO THE SEARCH

On your own, choose three occupations in the skilled professions to investigate. Go to the websites recommended by your teacher.

1. What does the Government of Canada Job Futures site say about future job prospects in these occupations?
2. What does the Ontario Job Futures site say about future job prospects in these occupations?
3. Is the information you learned about trends in your chosen occupations similar or different on these sites?
4. How can you explain the similarities and differences?
5. List four occupations these sites predict will have better future job prospects.
6. List four occupations these sites predict will have worse future job prospects.
7. Think about what you learned about trends in earlier chapters. Can you explain why some occupations seem to have better prospects and some have worse prospects?

Uniting for a Common Cause

As Canada has grown, the need for skilled workers has also grown. Canada has always relied on people who could build the things that communities need, including housing, roads, and vehicles.

In the early years of industrialization, workers had little job security, and also faced significant risk of on-the-job illness or injury. By joining together (uniting), individual workers formed organizations (**unions**) so that they could have more power negotiating with employers.

union
group of employees that negotiates with an employer about wages, benefits, and opportunities

The first *Trade Unions Act* in Canada was passed on June 14, 1872. Today, Canadian unions still represent the concerns of their members about

- wages and benefits (such as health and life insurance)
- working conditions (including their safety on the job)
- job security.

A LITTLE TOWN CALLED LITTLETOWN

Imagine that you work as a carpenter in a small, isolated town called Littletown. You work for the ABC Company, the only local company that employs carpenters. There are lots of carpenters around to take your job if you don't want it.

Now imagine that ABC can make more money if the boss tells the carpenters they must work an extra 10 hours per week for no extra pay. If you don't like the sound of this proposal, as an individual worker, your choices are limited:

- You can quit … but where will you find another job?
- You can argue … but why should they listen to you if they can easily hire someone who will agree to work the extra hours, possibly for even *less* pay?
- You can go along with the change … and any other change they make in the future.

Strikes have improved conditions for workers all across the country.

GO SMART … Uniting for a Common Cause

With a partner, think about the dilemma of a lone carpenter working for the ABC Company. Consider how different this situation would be if all of the carpenters in Littletown could

- join together to create a new organization (union) called Littletown United Carpenters
- sign an agreement that says no worker will work the extra hours unless they are all paid the same amount for this extra work
- stop working if the company refuses to pay them
- choose a representative to take this message to the ABC Company, and negotiate a settlement.

1. How might your situation as a carpenter at the ABC Company be different under these new circumstances?

2. How would this new situation change the balance of power between the ABC Company and the workers?

3. What might be the consequences if Littletown United Carpenters became very powerful?

4. How could the ABC Company lessen the power of the Littletown United Carpenters organization—maybe even convince the workers to dissolve their union?

SKILLS ○○○○○
STEPS ???○○

REAL-TIME RESUMÉ

How do I choose the first step?

Nargess knew she wanted to become a pastry chef the first time she baked in her grandmother's kitchen. She loved the feel of the dough in her hands and the smell of fruits, spices, and sugar bubbling away.

Her grandmother showed Nargess how to create light-as-air pastry as well as traditional Persian tarts and cookies. Nargess admired the way her grandmother's hands worked quickly and skilfully to turn the food into a work of art.

Now in her final year of high school, Nargess is committed more than ever to her goal of becoming the best pastry chef in the city. But she can't decide what her next step should be.

YOU BE THE COACH
Give Nargess your best reality check, using the tips below. Write your advice in the form of a magazine advice column.

REALITY CHECK

- Being great at something is just the beginning. Everyone needs a plan.

- Review this chapter to find three different ways to begin an apprenticeship program.

- Review the decision-making model in Chapter 3.

Read the Summary on page 85. Are there any ideas you are unsure of? Are there any skills you need to practise? If so, go back and review them.

 ... **Apprenticeship Programs**

 **DO THE SEARCH**

1. On your own, review what you have learned about apprenticeship programs.

2. Go to the websites recommended by your teacher.

3. Survey the occupations requiring an apprenticeship program (sometimes called "skilled trades").

4. Choose a few occupations to research more closely.

5. For each of these occupations, review the information, interviews, pictures, and videos provided to gather details that are important (jump back to research skills in Chapter 3).

6. Consider whether the apprenticeship style of learning is a good fit for you.

This chapter introduced you to the following ideas:

1. The skilled professions involve using your hands, body, and mind to build, fix, or create things.

2. Being in a skilled profession requires you to apprentice—that is, learn on the job with the help of a journeyperson.

3. Apprentices are paid on the job. One of the challenges of becoming an apprentice is finding the right company that is willing to help train you.

4. Co-op programs at high school, OYAP (the Ontario Youth Apprenticeship Program), and college programs are all roads that might lead you to a successful career in a skilled profession.

5. With the aging of the workforce, there will be many opportunities for young people who have apprenticed in a skilled profession.

6. Unions play an important role in the skilled professions. Unions lobby on behalf of their members for better working hours, benefits, and wages, and for worker safety, job security, and further learning.

Confident that you are ready to move forward?
Then go to the next adventure.

85

The Adventure: Post-Secondary Education

Decisions, Decisions ... But What's the Right One?

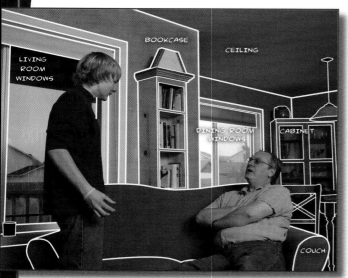

Many people will give you advice on what to do after high school ... but the ultimate decision is up to you!

Justin knew from the beginning of high school that his plan was to continue to higher learning. He had the marks, he was motivated, and he knew what interested him the most in terms of careers: industrial design.

After doing a lot of research on programs and touring colleges and universities, Justin found his dream program at the local college. The combination of hands-on, practical experience and theoretical learning definitely appealed to him the most.

However, Justin's dad disagreed.

"You're smart and you have strong marks. Why not go to university and study art and architecture?" his father asked after dinner one night. "You can go to college later if you want more hands-on."

Now Justin was stumped. He thought he'd chosen well. Did his dad have a point? Or was he stuck on university as the only acceptable post-secondary pathway?

- Why does Justin's father want him to go to university?
- What misconceptions does Justin's father seem to have about college?
- How would you handle the situation if your parents did not support your choice of college or university program?

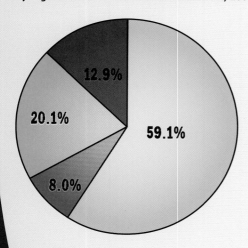

Canada's Population Aged 25 to 54
by Highest Level of Educational Attainment, 2004

- 12.9%
- 20.1%
- 59.1%
- 8.0%

- University degree or post-secondary certificate
- Some post-secondary
- High school diploma
- Less than high school

Source: Calculations by the Canadian Council on Social Development using data from Statistics Canada's *Historical Labour Force Review*, 2005, Cat. 71F0004XCB.

Remember to keep Tool 1 and Tool 2 handy. Watch for passions, preferences, and smarts that also describe you.

What's University All About?

University offers a wide variety of courses in every major discipline. The main purpose of university is to help you refine your higher-level thinking skills. As you explore your area of study more fully, you learn to think more critically and to analyze concepts in new ways.

University 101

+1 Universities are **degree**-granting institutions.

+2 They offer four-year programs to students with a high school diploma and at least six Grade 12 university prep courses, including any program prerequisites. Additional requirements may exist.

The $$ Factor

+1 University tuition is approximately $5000 to $8000 plus fees, books, and supplies (per year).

+2 Residence is available at an additional cost.

+3 **Bursaries** and **scholarships** are also available.

degree
title awarded by a university to a student who has completed a program of studies

bursary
award of money, usually based on financial need, that you do not have to pay back (see page 98)

scholarship
award of money, based on academic merit or other factors, that you do not have to pay back (see page 98)

undergraduate studies
studies pursued by students at a university who have not yet earned a degree

Bachelor's degree
first-level university degree (e.g., a Bachelor of Arts or of Science) in any discipline; below a Master's degree

University learning is theoretical and abstract. Only a few programs offer training for a specific job. For example, nursing, engineering, and business often integrate a co-operative education that provides experiential learning in the field. Most university programs, however, are deliberately general in nature.

When you leave high school and enter a university program, you begin your **undergraduate studies**. After four years of study, you obtain your undergraduate degree, known as a **Bachelor's degree**, in your subject area. You can specialize in one area or you can take a more general degree.

If this career adventure interests you, add that information to Tool 3. Review Tool 3 regularly and move the options that best fit you into the inner circle.

87

There are five areas of university studies:*

1. **Humanities**—English, Languages, Philosophy **Social Sciences**—History, Geography, Politics, Psychology, Sociology	**Bachelor of Arts (BA)**
2. **Life and Health Sciences**—Biology, Chemistry, Environmental Sciences, Kinesiology, Nursing	**Bachelor of Science (BSc)**
3. **Applied Sciences**—Engineering, Physics, Computer Science, Mathematics	**Bachelor of Applied Science (BASc) in designated field**
4. **Business and Commerce**—Accounting, Marketing, Business Finance	**Bachelor of Commerce (BComm) or Bachelor of Business Administration (BBA)**
5. **Fine Arts**—Visual Arts, Music, Film Studies, Theatre Arts	**Bachelor of Fine Arts (BFA)**

* Note: Institutions may use different designations to identify their Bachelor's degree programs.

Master's degree
university degree ranking above a Bachelor's degree (in any discipline)

Doctor of Philosophy (PhD)
university degree ranking above a Master's degree (in any discipline), involving original research and a thesis

Once you have your Bachelor's degree, you may wish to continue on to do graduate studies and to complete your **Master's degree**. After this, if you are really interested in doing more research in your area of study, you may decide to go for your **Doctor of Philosophy (PhD)**.

Occupations Requiring University

- Medicine and dentistry
- Pharmacy
- Accounting and auditing
- Computer programming
- Engineering
- Architecture
- Law
- Library science
- Teaching
- Veterinary medicine

Interested in these occupations? University is required for each one.

GO SMART ... University Programs

1. Using pages 87–88, as well as materials and tips provided by your teacher, see if you can find the answers to these questions. Use the accompanying line master to record your information.

   - What are the admission requirements for Ontario universities?
   - What is the average course load (number of courses) of an undergraduate student?
   - Give an example of a first-year course in each of the five areas of university studies shown above (can be from any Ontario university).

   - What are the total annual student expenses for a first-year undergraduate student living in residence at the University of Ottawa?
   - What is the Ontario Universities Fair and why should interested students attend?

2. Compile a list of university programs that might be of interest to you using the same materials provided by your teacher.

Being at University

**Cassandra,
University of Guelph**

Cassandra's latest blog entry

When I was growing up, I always enjoyed science—particularly the units on earth sciences. I even read my science book in my spare time!

In high school, I got involved in the Environment Club and eventually became president. We created campaigns like "Turn-Off-the-Lights Fridays," organized rallies against idling cars during morning drop-off, and started petitions to save local conservation areas.

What began as a social club grew into a real passion for me. Today, I'm studying Environmental Governance at the University of Guelph. The program focuses on teaching students how to safeguard the environment through innovative approaches to governing. I hope to get into local policy making one day so that I can contribute more fully to my local community and to educate the public about environmental issues.

Universities expect their staff to keep on learning too. If you love hanging out with people who love ideas and discovering new things, university might be for you. Pictured here: Professor Robert Reisz (left) of the University of Toronto and Professor James Kitching (right) of the University of the Witwatersrand in Johannesburg, who recently discovered two 190-million-year-old dinosaur embryos in South Africa.

There are many extracurricular activities to choose from at university—you just have to find the one that's right for you. Here, Brock University students in St. Catharines, Ontario participate in a community cleanup, the Adopt a Road Super Saturday, to show their commitment to the environment.

an article by Jeff Rybak

Why Go to University? Some Students Don't Have a Clue

There are a shocking number of students in university who would be stunned by the idea that one needs a reason to be there. For them, there are things in life you just don't question.

At some stage, you finish Grade 8, and the next year a bus comes and takes you to high school. You don't ask why, you just go. And in many cases, the transition to university is managed just as smoothly by parents, friends, and surrounding people who always assumed it would happen. You don't ask why, you just fill out your applications, maybe sign the loan documents, and go.

What's College All About?

College offers affordable, practical, hands-on preparation for "real" jobs. The main purpose of college is to provide you with the knowledge and skills necessary for a specific field of work. You'll get lots of practical experience in this setting for whatever it is you want to do.

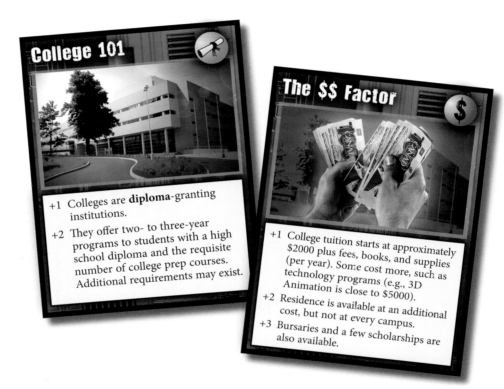

College 101

+1 Colleges are **diploma**-granting institutions.

+2 They offer two- to three-year programs to students with a high school diploma and the requisite number of college prep courses. Additional requirements may exist.

The $$ Factor

+1 College tuition starts at approximately $2000 plus fees, books, and supplies (per year). Some cost more, such as technology programs (e.g., 3D Animation is close to $5000).

+2 Residence is available at an additional cost, but not at every campus.

+3 Bursaries and a few scholarships are also available.

diploma
document granted by a college to show academic achievement in a particular field of study

The traditional college program entered from high school is called a diploma program. It varies in length depending on the job that it is preparing you for, but the program will usually take you two to three years to complete.

certificate
document granted by a college to a student who has completed a specific field of study (e.g., elevator mechanic)

Colleges also run **certificate** programs that are shorter in length—usually completed in one year. The major advantage of college training is that it often includes job placements, internships, field placements, and co-op opportunities that allow you to build your skills while you earn valuable work experience.

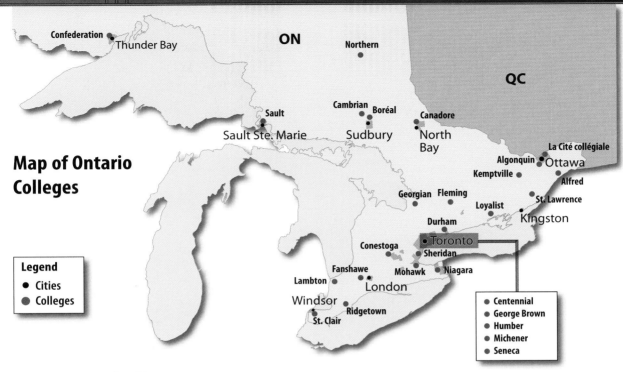

Map of Ontario Colleges

ON

QC

Confederation • Thunder Bay

Northern •

Sault • Sault Ste. Marie

Cambrian • Boréal

Sudbury

Canadore • North Bay

La Cité collégiale

Algonquin • Ottawa

Kemptville •

Alfred •

Georgian • Fleming

St. Lawrence

Loyalist • Kingston

Durham •

Conestoga • Toronto

Sheridan •

Fanshawe •

Mohawk • Niagara •

Lambton •

London

Windsor

Ridgetown •

St. Clair

Legend
- • Cities
- • Colleges

- • Centennial
- • George Brown
- • Humber
- • Michener
- • Seneca

Being at College

Dave, George Brown College, Toronto

Dave's latest blog entry

I've always loved hotels. When I was growing up, my uncle owned a resort in Muskoka, Ontario. I used to hang out there every summer, helping to tend to the guests and working at the front desk when I got older. Even my favourite shows on television always seem to have hotels in them!

In school I'd never thought seriously about pursuing my interest as a career goal, but as I neared high school graduation, I started to do some research about hospitality courses. I found that there were some really great programs out there. I finally decided to apply to George Brown College in Toronto and take the Hotel Management program.

Because of my part-time experience and recommendation letters from my uncle and my teachers, I got in! It's a lot of hard work but I love it!

Checklist

Is college right for me?

- ◯ I learn best by doing.
- ◯ I enjoy learning practical things that I can apply to my life.
- ◯ I want to get specialized training for a specific job.
- ◯ I do not want to "break the bank" getting my education.
- ◯ I do not want to spend much more time in school.

Colleges are always adding to their program offerings. As the business world expands, so do they. St. Clair College in Windsor, Ontario, for example, was the first to offer an entertainment technology course based on the growing need for touring sound and lighting technicians and project managers in the entertainment industry.

DO THE SEARCH ▶

GO SMART ... College Programs

1. What are the admission requirements for Ontario college diploma programs?
2. Using the Venn diagram line master provided by your teacher, compare university and college for the following factors:
   - admission requirements
   - length of program
   - type of program
   - tuition expenses
   - residence
   - scholarships
   - accreditation (degree, diploma, certificate) upon graduation.
3. Compile a list of college programs that might be of interest to you using the resources provided by your teacher.

College/University Hybrids: The Best of Both Worlds?

Today there are many opportunities to pursue both the university and the college experience. Why not go for a joint or applied degree program? You get the best of both worlds—the theoretical learning of university along with the hands-on, job-specific training of college. In the end, you will hold both a university degree and a college diploma! Sounds like a pretty appealing choice, doesn't it? Check out your options!

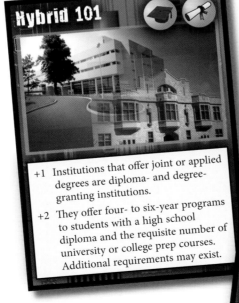

Hybrid 101

+1 Institutions that offer joint or applied degrees are diploma- and degree-granting institutions.

+2 They offer four- to six-year programs to students with a high school diploma and the requisite number of university or college prep courses. Additional requirements may exist.

The $$ Factor

+1 Tuition expenses for a joint program are approximately $5000 plus fees, books, and supplies (per year).

+2 Residence is available at an additional cost.

+3 Bursaries and scholarships are also available.

JOINT OR COLLABORATIVE PROGRAM

This program allows you to take both college and university courses at the same time in order to complete both a diploma and a degree in your area of study. You must have the prerequisite high school university preparatory courses to apply.

APPLIED DEGREE PROGRAM

This program is usually housed at the college. It is a university degree that combines theory and practical, hands-on learning. This degree provides specialized training for a specific job. You must have the prerequisite high school university preparatory courses to apply.

DEGREE COMPLETION PROGRAM

Some students are not quite ready to enter into a university program from high school. In this case, you may start in a college diploma program, and move into a university program within the same subject area through a college-university transfer agreement. In the end, you will end up with both a diploma and a degree.

You must have the prerequisite high school college preparatory courses to apply for the college diploma program. Your college grade point average (GPA) will determine your eligibility for the degree completion at university.

Continuing with post-secondary education involves a lot of work—but everything that you put into it will serve you in the future.

Danielle, Lambton College-Lakehead University

Danielle's latest blog entry

When I was in high school, I always worked as a camp counsellor during the summer. I really like working with kids and helping them learn how to solve their own problems. My main goal was always to get out of school as quickly as possible and start working!

I didn't have lots of money so I chose to complete the two-year Social Worker Service Program at Lambton College. When I finished the program, I was immediately hired in the local school where I completed my field work. I worked there for three years and decided that in order to make a little more money in my field, I would need to go to university.

It turned out that Lakehead University would accept my diploma courses toward completing my degree in social work. My degree has now changed my role—from child and youth worker to social worker—which allows me to help my students in new ways. I am still doing what I am passionate about, and I'm getting better pay!

Checklist

Is a college/university hybrid right for me?

- ○ I learn best by doing, hearing, and seeing.
- ○ I enjoy practical, real-life experiences combined with theoretical learning.
- ○ I am interested in pursuing specific job training.
- ○ I would like to have both a college diploma and a university degree.
- ○ I am willing to invest both time and money for the education that is best for me.

GO SMART ... Hybrid Programs

1. List the three hybrid college-university programs, and describe each one briefly.

2. How did the collaborative program at Lambton College-Lakehead University open new doors for Danielle?

3. Using the *Work Smart* sections on university, college, and hybrid programs as a guide (pages 87–93), create your own 8½ × 11 two-fold brochure about these three options. List the advantages, cost, and important details for each option.

4. How would you advise someone who cannot decide between all-university and all-college or a hybrid program? Develop some questions to ask that person to help him or her decide.

Private Career Colleges

Wise Words

"Intelligence plus character —that is the goal of true education."

—*Martin Luther King Jr., American civil rights leader*

Private career colleges offer a wide range of programs that provide specialized training for specific jobs. They are for-profit organizations, and are therefore more costly than publicly funded colleges. For example, Accounting at Seneca College, a two-year program, will cost approximately $5000. Accounting at Everest College (private), a seven-month program, will cost approximately $10,000. Private colleges tend to offer a lot of the same kinds of programs as the traditional colleges, but some are exclusive to private colleges.

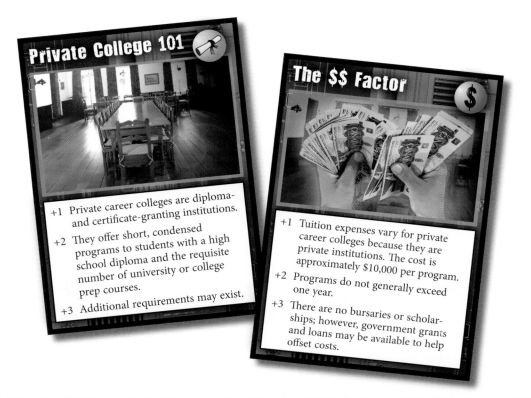

Private College 101

+1 Private career colleges are diploma- and certificate-granting institutions.

+2 They offer short, condensed programs to students with a high school diploma and the requisite number of university or college prep courses.

+3 Additional requirements may exist.

The $$ Factor

+1 Tuition expenses vary for private career colleges because they are private institutions. The cost is approximately $10,000 per program.

+2 Programs do not generally exceed one year.

+3 There are no bursaries or scholarships; however, government grants and loans may be available to help offset costs.

There are many highly specialized private career colleges in Ontario. Do some research and find out if one of them is right for you!

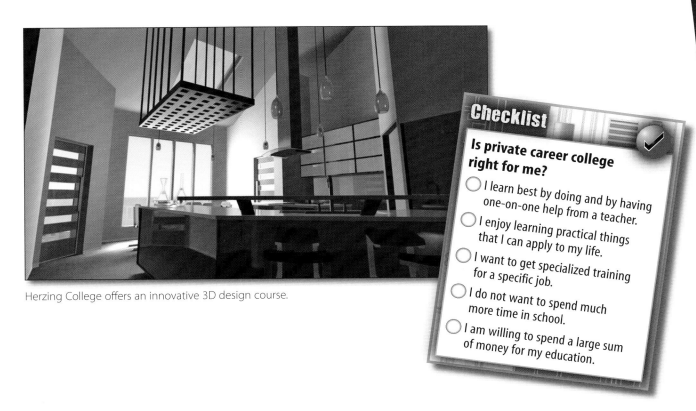

Herzing College offers an innovative 3D design course.

Checklist

Is private career college right for me?

○ I learn best by doing and by having one-on-one help from a teacher.

○ I enjoy learning practical things that I can apply to my life.

○ I want to get specialized training for a specific job.

○ I do not want to spend much more time in school.

○ I am willing to spend a large sum of money for my education.

GO SMART ... Private Career College Programs

1. Investigate private colleges in Ontario and find three programs offered at private colleges that are not yet offered anywhere else.

2. On at least two or three private college websites, try to ascertain why one might choose a private college over a public college. What do these institutions claim is their advantage?

3. Imagine you were to start up a private college in your area. What specific courses would you offer that students cannot find anywhere else? or at least nowhere else that is close by?

4. Why might college teachers prefer private institutions over public colleges? Try to back up your reasons with statistical information (salaries for staff, student success rates).

DO THE SEARCH

Step 37(c): Point ROCKET(B) at PLANET(F), and light FUSE(G).
* NOTE: Remember to open WINDOW(K).
? TIP: Did you pack a snack?

Rocket Science: The online course
www.betsystreeter.com

Online courses offer students the flexibility to learn independently.

Distance Education

If you are looking for a non-traditional way to complete your post-secondary studies, distance education, including online learning, may be for you. Many institutions provide a variety of programs through distance education. Try the checklist below to see if it's right for you!

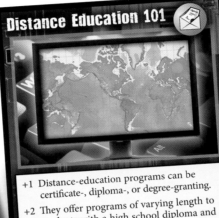

Distance Education 101

+1 Distance-education programs can be certificate-, diploma-, or degree-granting.

+2 They offer programs of varying length to students with a high school diploma and the requisite number of university or college prep courses.

+3 Programs are delivered through either correspondence or email. Distance education resolves the problem of people living in remote areas having to commute to go to school.

The $$ Factor

+1 Tuition expenses vary, depending on the program and the number of credits taken.

+2 One credit costs $140; up to nine credits costs $1,441.

+3 There are no bursaries or scholarships; however, government grants and loans may be available to help offset costs.

Checklist

Is distance education right for me?

○ I learn best independently.

○ I enjoy learning at my own pace.

○ I am self-motivated.

○ I am looking for a non-traditional classroom environment.

○ I want to get my education while working, travelling, or raising a family.

GO SMART ... PMI About Distance Education

Use the line master provided by your teacher to complete a Plus, Minus, Interesting chart for distance education. Consider the advantages of online learning (the Plus), the disadvantages (the Minus), and some specific details about distance education that you'd like to know more about (the Interesting).

Plus, Minus, Interesting Chart for Distance Education

Plus	Minus	Interesting

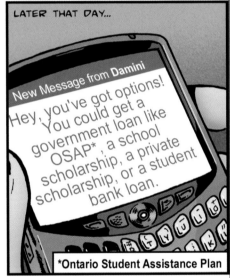

1. VISIT THE GOVERNMENT OF CANADA'S CANLEARN WEBSITE. CLICK ONLINE TOOLS, CLICK PLANNERS AND CALCULATORS, SELECT FINANCIAL PLANNER, AND ESTIMATE THE COST OF YOUR COLLEGE OR UNIVERSITY EDUCATION. THEN CREATE A BUDGET.

2. WHILE YOU ARE AT THE CANLEARN WEBSITE, CLICK ON POST-SECONDARY AND REVIEW THE SECTION CALLED MONEY FOR SCHOOL. USING THE INFORMATION ON THE WEBSITE, CREATE A FINANCIAL PLAN FOR PETER TO HELP HIM PAY FOR HIS POST-SECONDARY EDUCATION.

Financing Your Education

Here's what you need to know about financing your post-secondary education.

"If you miss a payment, we show up and embarrass you in front of your friends."

Paying off your student loan will be made easier if you make the right career choice after graduation.

GOVERNMENT LOAN

Loans from the provincial government such as the Ontario Student Assistance Plan (OSAP) help students pay for their post-secondary education and must be paid back over a period of time. Government loans typically offer a low-interest payback period.

GRANT OR BURSARY

A **grant** or bursary is a set amount of money that is usually awarded to students based on financial need. You do not have to pay back this money.

SCHOLARSHIP

This money is typically awarded based on academic merit or other factors such as leadership experience and school or community involvement. You do not have to pay this money back.

STUDENT BANK LOAN/LINE OF CREDIT

These are funds you receive from the bank that must be paid back over a period of time. Financial institutions such as banks will often offer lower interest rates and different payback periods for students.

grant
award of money, usually based on financial need, that you do not have to pay back

Post-secondary education can be expensive, but it will open up many doors.

Read the Summary on page 99. Are there any ideas you are unsure of? Are there any skills you need to practise? If so, go back and review them.

 ... **Post-Secondary Blog Profile**

1. Create your own blog entry similar to the student blog entries on pages 89, 91, and 93 and send it to a friend or relative, bringing them up to date about you. Talk about your interests and areas of strength, and where you might be headed based on your self-knowledge. Outline at least two possible post-secondary options.

2. On the line master distributed by your teacher, complete the information about each of your options, including name of the university, college, or other institution; location; prerequisite courses; mark cut-off range; and any other admission information.

3. With information provided by your teacher, go to the Government of Canada's Education Cost Calculator and use it to figure out how much each of your options is going to cost. The Cost Calculator will ask you all the right questions. The only information you need is

   ● the institution you plan on attending
   ● the program name
   ● the year you plan to start.

   Use the Loan Repayment Calculator to figure out how long it would take to pay back a loan for your education.

DO THE SEARCH

This chapter introduced you to the following ideas:

1. University is a good choice for students wishing to continue their education without too much career-related specialization. It's ideal for those wishing to develop their higher-level thinking skills.

2. College is a good choice for students who learn better using a hands-on approach and for those who already have a good idea of the line of work they would like to get into.

3. Hybrid programs are now available to students who wish to earn a university degree and a college diploma. The benefit of such programs is that you have the flexibility of choosing between university AND college courses.

4. Private career colleges offer high-end, specialized training in streamlined programs that get you into the workforce as fast as possible.

5. Distance education is a flexible way to continue your education while working, travelling, or even raising a family.

6. Whatever your choice for post-secondary education, tuition is always an issue. You must consider how much you are willing to invest in your education versus how much you will get out of it, which, in most cases, will be a lot!

Confident that you are ready to move forward?
Then go to the next chapter.

99

PART 3:

MORE TOOLS OF THE TRADE

In this part of *Work Smart*, you will have the opportunity to

- use different resources to apply for part-time jobs in your community or a summer job
- brush up on your resumé and cover-letter skills
- learn how to complete a job application
- practise preparing for job interviews using role plays and other strategies
- get acquainted with a variety of non-verbal communication techniques such as "the perfect handshake" and good body language

- research the education, training, and skill requirements of specific occupations
- sensitize yourself to the importance of diversity on the job
- demonstrate how teamwork and leadership can help to address conflict

The Get-Out-of-School Plan

Now What?

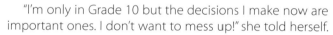

Jenny was feeling overwhelmed.

At this stage, she had a better idea of where she was headed after high school but she still felt nervous about making it happen. Though excited about her future prospects, she didn't want to make any mistakes.

"I'm only in Grade 10 but the decisions I make now are important ones. I don't want to mess up!" she told herself.

Do you sympathize with Jenny? You're not alone. Turns out, all her friends felt the same way. Everyone was anxious about making good decisions now that Grade 11 was looming.

RELAX! All Jenny needs to do is a little bit of planning. Let's take a closer look at where Jenny is in order to see what her next steps might be.

- Jenny has gotten to know herself a little better. She understands her interests, her strengths, and her challenges.
- Jenny has figured out some possible options for after high school.
- Jenny has learned what she needs to do to get out of high school.
- Jenny has practised decision-making skills and can now apply them to planning for her future.

So, what's next? How is Jenny going to get to her preferred post-secondary destination?

The answer is simple: The Get-Out-of-School Plan!

- Have you ever felt like Jenny?
- Have you had a goal before and not been able to make it happen? What got in the way?
- Have you had a goal and been successful in making it happen? What steps did you take to make sure you achieved your goal?

Throughout this chapter, record what courses you may need to take for some of the fields of work and occupations you have identified using Tool 2.

Shekufe plans on going to college.

Start here. Go anywhere!

APPRENTICESHIP   REAL JOB

YOUR OWN BUSINESS

UNIVERSITY   COLLEGE

TRAVEL   VOLUNTEER

STAY IN   HIGH SCHOOL

Anuar wants to be a helicopter mechanic.

Dustin would like to teach.

Katryn wants to run her own store one day.

Think, "What could I do today, tomorrow, and the next day to find out what I need to do to get closer to one of the occupations that I am interested in?"

Those Who Fail to Plan, Plan to Fail

In order to get where you want to go, you need to make a plan. Of course, you have been planning throughout this course. In Parts 1 and 2 of *Work Smart*, you have been busy figuring out where you might be headed based on the options available.

Now, you need to do some short-term and long-term planning to make sure it all comes together successfully.

WHAT YOU NEED TO GRADUATE

Selecting courses to match your strengths (see Chapter 2) and knowing about graduation requirements will help you get on the path to success.

SELECTING YOUR COURSES

The key to course selection is having a plan. You need to know

- what courses you must take in order to graduate or qualify for a post-secondary program (**required courses**)
- what courses lead to more advanced courses (**prerequisites**)
- what courses you could take to suit your strengths and interests (**options**).

Usually, there is a special time at school to make course selections for the following year. To help you decide which courses to take, your school may offer a booklet (course directory) or a website that describes course offerings. Sometimes, you will be asked to input your course selections directly into a computer program.

Start planning your course selections by identifying the required courses you have not yet earned. Most schools can provide you with a **Credit Counselling Summary**, which lists the courses you have already completed and shows you the courses that you still need to take.

required courses
courses you need to take and pass in order to graduate

prerequisites
courses you need to take and pass before enrolling in other courses

options
courses you can choose to take; these courses are not mandatory to graduate from high school

credit
recognition for successfully completing a course; you need 30 credits to graduate from high school

Credit Counselling Summary
tool used to track courses students have taken and those they need to take in order to graduate

Making the right course selections will help you with your Get-Out-of-School plan.

A teacher or guidance counsellor may be able to answer your questions about picking the right courses. You can also talk to your parents and older siblings about course selection as well. There are also many websites to assist Ontario students with course planning. Your teacher can share these resources with you.

Top 5 Ways to Get Where You Want to Go

DO THE SEARCH

1. Start early—plan out your courses.
2. Keep a personal profile (report cards, awards, volunteer hours, record of club or team participation).
3. Research post-secondary options (prerequisites for programs).
4. Know whom to ask for help (teachers, counsellors, parents).
5. Never give up! Perseverance is key!

GO SMART ... Making Your Own Course Plan

1. Use the information you collected about yourself in Parts 1 and 2 of *Work Smart* to think about what you would really like to study. This is not a question you need to answer in five seconds. Mull it over. Ask other students or a teacher for their input.

2. Examine …

   DO THE SEARCH
   - The Ontario Ministry of Education requirements to graduate. You may be able to review the work you completed in Chapter 3. Alternatively, your teacher will direct you to the appropriate print material or website.

   DO THE SEARCH
   - Other courses you could take—options—to suit your strengths and interests. Find this information in your school's course directory or on the school website.

3. Track your required courses using the line master provided by your teacher. Use your Credit Counselling Summary to help you identify which required courses you have already earned and those you still need.

4. Now try filling out a chart similar to the one on the next page or using the line master provided by your teacher. (Alternatively, your school might have its own template for you to use.) This chart allows you to fill in the courses you have already taken and to plan for your next two years of high school. If you make this chart yourself, add a sixth column where your post-secondary destination prerequisite courses can be entered. That way, you will know what courses you need to take in Grades 11 and 12 to get to your destination.

5. A non-academic requirement to graduate is 40 community involvement hours, such as volunteer work.

   a) What types of volunteer work do you do or have an interest in doing?

   b) List examples of volunteer work you see in this chapter or in other sections of *Work Smart*. Which ones appeal to you?

   c) How could you best plan to accumulate these hours between now and graduation?

   The Credits Chart is on the next page.

GO SMART ... Making Your Own Course Plan (continued)

CREDITS CHART   Compulsory credits (18) + optional credits (12) = 30 credits total

Subject and Compulsory Credits	Grade 9	Grade 10	Grade 11	Grade 12
English, 4 credits	English	English	English	English
Mathematics, 3 credits	Mathematics	Mathematics	Mathematics	—
Science, 2 credits	Science	Science	—	—
French, 1 credit	French	—	—	—
Canadian Geography, 1 credit	Geography	—	—	—
Canadian History, 1 credit	—	History	—	—
Health and Physical Education, 1 credit	Health and Physical Education	—	—	—
Arts, 1 credit	—	Music	—	—
Civics and Career Studies, 1 credit	—	Civics/Career	—	—
1 additional credit from **Group 1**	—	—	—	—
1 additional credit from **Group 2**	—	—	—	—
1 additional credit from **Group 3**	—	—	—	—

Group 1   1 additional credit in English OR additional credit in French as a Second Language OR Classical or an International Language OR Native Language OR Social Science and Humanities credit OR Canada and World Studies credit OR Guidance and Career Education credit OR Co-operative Education credit*

Group 2   1 additional Health and Physical Education credit OR additional Arts credit OR Business Studies credit OR Co-operative Education credit*

Group 3   1 additional Science credit OR Technological Education credit OR Co-operative Education credit*

*   A maximum of 2 credits in Co-operative Education can count as compulsory credits.
In addition to 30 credits (including 18 compulsory credits), don't forget that you must successfully complete the Ontario Secondary School Literacy Test and 40 hours of community involvement.

1. CREATE A PLAN TO HELP YOU PREPARE FOR COURSE SELECTION BY WRITING DOWN THE STEPS YOU NEED TO TAKE TO ENSURE THAT YOUR CHOICE OF COURSES IS RIGHT FOR YOU.

2. HOW CAN A WEBSITE LIKE MYBLUEPRINT HELP YOU MAKE COURSE-SELECTION DECISIONS?

3. IDENTIFY THREE PEOPLE YOU CAN TALK TO IF YOU GET STUCK IN MAKING YOUR COURSE SELECTIONS.

Kendra likes visiting with an elderly neighbour. Could that be part of her community service?

Making a Difference in Your Community

After planning her courses for Grades 11 and 12, Kendra is feeling less stressed out about the future. She knows which courses she needs to take and which options she can fit in. Whew!

Now the only thing left to plan for is the completion of her community involvement hours. Kendra knows that there are many opportunities available to her but she does not know where to start. Then she comes across the following article in the local newspaper.

Fundraising, such as organizing a car wash at your school to raise money for a cause or campaign, is a great way to get involved in the community!

non-governmental organization (NGO)
non-profit group that works on a specific cause that is not funded or managed by the government (e.g., the World Wildlife Fund)

global citizenship
belief that all citizens of the world are responsible for each other and for the planet

40 hours of community involvement:
Diploma requirement or a life-changing experience?

Sunita Singh was only 15 when she founded a club at her school aimed at raising money and awareness for a **non-government organization (NGO)** helping community development projects in underserviced areas of northern Peru.

It all started in her Grade 10 year while taking her Civics compulsory credit. In her class, she learned the importance of **global citizenship** while working with Para el Mundo, a Toronto-based NGO, which helps out in the small community of Mancora, Peru.

Sunita's class assisted the organization by holding bake sales to raise money and by asking local business and community members for donations to help support their cause. In the end, the fundraising was very successful and Sunita's class was able to purchase enough books to start a community after-school reading program.

At the end of the semester, Sunita earned her Civics credit but she felt that there was still more that she could do for Para el Mundo. As part of the Ontario Secondary School Diploma (OSSD) requirement, students must complete 40 hours of community involvement. In the past, Sunita felt that it was a waste of time.

"Why couldn't I just get a job and start saving money rather than volunteering?" she remembers thinking.

Sunita did not want to volunteer just because she was told to do so. However, her work with Para el Mundo changed her way of thinking. She was able to make a real contribution and see that a community needed her help. She felt really good at the end of her class project knowing that she was able to make a difference in the lives of others.

"I never had the intention of creating a committee at my school linked to a charity or even getting involved in the area of international aid," she says. But her work with her class led her down that path.

—Continued on page 9.

—In ulluptatie vulland

In ulluptatie vulland iamcon utpat. Pis deliqui pismodigna feui et amcon vent ut vulput la aliquisisi tin ut laorero conse faccumsandre commy nullute modolum dolore faciduis nostio dit et aco

Lute fi
nos non
iure mag

Met in
delenisi.

Et nulla
esto cor
blandit v
ndigna a
sum adig

Omm,
dolore e
vel eseq

Uscili
del ing e
sismod e
sit alisci
et, volor
luptat, q
delis nis
Ignisl in
tat.

Ing ex
quat. Ut
eugiame
aliquam
conums;
tatem ni
et erilla
hendion

Lor se
Facil dol

—*Continued from page 5.*

Sunita, now 17 and getting closer to earning her high school diploma, intends to continue her work with Para el Mundo to complete her community involvement hours. She will likely contribute many more hours than the 40 required for graduation.

As a result of her involvement with this NGO, Sunita has decided to pursue International Development in her post-secondary studies. She plans to save enough money to eventually visit the town of Mancora in order to see the fruits of her labour.

Does she see herself as a global citizen?

"Social responsibility starts right here," she says. "You don't have to leave your local community to take action. Something as simple as helping a neighbour can make our world a better place."

For Sunita, the key to contributing to society is to be passionate about your goals and your ideals. She encourages her peers to get involved in organizations that interest them to

Earth Day, April 22, marks the anniversary of the birth of the modern environmental movement in 1970. Volunteers and activists (many students) around the world show their commitment to protecting the environment through projects and cleanups.

complete their community involvement hours.

"I always thought that I would complete my 40 hours and end it there, but now I see the value of getting more involved in my community."

Sunita is just one of the growing numbers of Canadian youth trying to make a difference. Today, more and more young people are taking matters into their own hands and starting their own charities and clubs, whether at school or in the community. They believe in the power of volunteerism to gain new experiences, new skills, and a whole new outlook on life. ◆

9

GO SMART ... The Benefits of Community Involvement

1. a) How did Sunita get involved with Para el Mundo?

   b) How might community involvement help you direct your education and future career path, as it did with Sunita?

2. a) Describe how volunteer work might help you gain experience and confidence that can carry over to future jobs.

   b) What about making contacts? How can volunteer contacts help you in the future?

3. Prepare a short-term plan to get involved. What steps will you take to do this? Use the line master distributed by your teacher to complete this task.

4. What effect do you think community involvement can have on your long-term goals?

5. What other resources could you use to find out more about community involvement opportunities?

Be Proactive! Be Your Own Self-Advocate!

Does it seem to you that some people are always lucky? They always get what they want and things always seem to go their way.

Maybe they are not lucky; maybe they are just excellent **advocates** for themselves. Self-advocacy means:

advocates
people who speak up for a cause, for others, or for themselves

- knowing yourself and knowing what you need
- knowing who can help you
- being able to ask someone for what you need.

Wise Words

"Luck is when opportunity meets preparedness."

—*Old saying*

To be a good self-advocate, you must be able to do all three things. When creating your Get-Out-of-School Plan, you need to use these steps too. Remember that in order to get where you want to go, you may need to ask for help. So long as you know what you need and who can guide you through the process, you will find more success.

No one is going to live your life for you, but there are people who can assist you. Take charge!

Steps to Self-Advocacy

1. You need something
▼
2. You realize that someone has what you need
▼
3. You ask for help in an appropriate way

Everyone needs help at some point. Sometimes, you need to ask a teacher for extra input or advice on an assignment.

GO SMART ... Self-Advocacy Situations

1. a) With a partner, look over the two situations below in which you might advocate for yourself.
    - Situation A: with a teacher or guidance counsellor (to plot your courses)
    - Situation B: with potential community service contacts (to find a volunteer project that suits you)

    Keep your Get-Out-of-School plan in mind as your brainstorm these situations.

    b) For Situation A, use the chart below to organize how you will advocate for yourself in choosing your courses with the help of a teacher or guidance counsellor.

Situation	What I Need	Who Can Help Me	How I Would Prepare

    c) For Situation B, use the same chart or adjust it to help you approach potential community service contacts to find a volunteer project that suits you.

2. With a partner, choose one of the two situations. Prepare a role play in which you advocate for yourself in an appropriate way.

3. Experts say that people who write down their goals are more likely to achieve them and find success. Keep notes on either Situation A: what courses to take or Situation B: which community service project to volunteer with.

REAL-TIME RESUMÉ

Help, I'm a bit lost!

ENERGY ⚪⚪⚪⚪⚪
PLAN ⑦●●●●

Cameron always liked school. He filled up his spares in high school with extra courses. He took summer school—not to make up his marks, but because he loves learning and studying so much. He has just finished Grade 12, and all of a sudden he is feeling a bit lost.

He has applied to a few universities and has been accepted, but his real passion is his music, and he is not sure that university is the path for him. He has a summer job lined up, but what should he do in September?

Cameron is feeling a bit overwhelmed and a bit depressed. He doesn't really want to have to decide what to do with this life at 17! His friends are all planning what they will do next year—and they all seem excited. He doesn't feel that he can talk to any of them about this feeling of being a bit lost. His younger sister is great but she can't really help with the way he is feeling about his future. His parents wouldn't understand—they are just thrilled that he got into the universities he applied to.

What should he do?

YOU BE THE COACH

If you were Cameron's best friend, what advice would you give him? Give Cameron three good options for his situation based on what you know of him, and what you have learned so far in *Work Smart*. Role-play this conversation with another student acting as Cameron.

REALITY CHECK

- Some students may want to take a year off to work or travel. If in doubt, a school guidance counsellor can help.

- Students can stay in high school for another semester or apply for co-op. They can use this time to figure out what they would like to do.

- Part-time jobs or volunteer programs in an area of interest can give students hands-on experience and help them decide what's right for them.

STILL DON'T KNOW WHERE TO GO NEXT?

Consider other options …

Katimavik is a federal government program in which young people aged 17 to 21 spend 9 months helping in community projects in three different areas of Canada. Katimavik offers young Canadians an exciting experience that incorporates learning and volunteer involvement.

Class Afloat is a unique Canadian boarding school on a sailing ship offering high school and first-year college programs. Students learn on board while they travel around the world. Not only does this adventure allow students to continue their education, it gives them first-hand experience on a tall ship, and all the benefits of travelling.

International Student Exchange programs offer students the opportunity to experience a new culture, become fluent in another language, and make new friends to last a lifetime! Where do you want to spend your high school year abroad? Some students even decide to finish up their Grade 12 here, and then go to another country for a year.

Wise Words

"Learning is like rowing upstream: not to advance is to drop back."

—*Chinese saying*

Katimavik is a hands-on volunteer work experience that teaches young people invaluable skills such as teamwork and project organization.

Read the Summary on page 113. Are there any ideas you are unsure of? Are there any skills you need to practise? If so, go back and review them.

This chapter introduced you to the following ideas:

1. Getting out of high school is your next big goal. Some students feel over-whelmed about what to do after graduation. The best solution is to come up with a good plan.

2. After high school, there are so many options: university, college, an appren-ticeship, starting up your own business, or your first "real" job. Start to do some long-term planning while you are still in high school.

3. Selecting your courses is a very important step in your Get-Out-of-School plan. See a guidance counsellor. Fill in a planning chart (either the *Work Smart* chart or one provided by your school). Know what you will need to graduate and go from there!

4. Figure out which compulsory credits you will need first, and fill in that part of your planning chart. Next, look at all the optional credits you would like. Can you fit them all in? Are you headed in the right direction for what you might like to do after high school?

5. Another graduation requirement is 40 hours of community service. This is your chance to volunteer in an area that interests you, gain experience, and make some invaluable contacts.

6. Don't forget the Grade 10 Literacy Test. You must pass it to graduate.

7. Know what you want or need—and go get it! Being a good advocate for yourself means knowing your needs, finding people to help, and then asking for help in an appropriate way.

Confident that you are ready to move forward?
Then go to the next chapter.

113

Winning Resumés, Cover Letters, and Applications

10 Seconds to Impress: Would You Make the Cut?

Paul knows what he is looking for— winning resumés!

Paul is a **resumé** reviewer for a large company in Toronto. Whenever his company advertises a position, they usually get between 800 and 1000 applicants. Paul's job is to reduce that number down to a pool of about 30 resumés that will be read more closely. How does he read through 1000 resumés?

The answer is, he doesn't. Paul, like other reviewers, scans each application for about 10 seconds.

"If the resumé is in a fancy font, or longer than two pages, I don't even scan it," he admits. "If the cover letter isn't addressed to someone in the company, or just quotes the job ad, I don't even get to the resumé. It may seem harsh, but I eliminate anyone whose writing contains spelling or grammar mistakes."

"The key to surviving the first cut is to show the employer that you have put the effort into researching and editing your work. I can usually get rid of about half of the applicants before I even start to scan for key words and skills."

resumé

summary of all of your education, job, volunteer, and other accomplishments and experiences; a resumé is often called a curriculum vitæ or a C.V.

- What are the most important ways to make a good first impression with your application, cover letter, and resumé?
- How could you find out more detailed information about a company for your cover letter?
- How can you make sure your resumé is error-free before sending it to a company?

Review your passions, preferences, and smarts from Tool 1. Is there anything else to add?

Your Resumé

Your resumé is your chance to show the employer the knowledge and skills you have and how you acquired them. Don't panic if you haven't had a lot of paid employment; you can highlight your **transferable skills** from volunteer work and other experiences.

transferable skills

skills acquired in any area of life that can be applied to other situations, including a job

PERSONAL INFORMATION

On your resumé, you must include information about where you live and where you can be reached. Generally, this means your

- name
- street address
- email address (provided that you check it regularly)
- telephone number.

EDUCATION

Your resumé should tell the person reading it how much schooling you have had. State what grade you are in or have just completed. Mention any courses you have taken outside school (such as first aid or music training).

Resumé

A. Student

123 Happy Lane
Anytown, ON A0A 0B1

416-123-4567
905-891-0123 (cellular)
astudent123@resume.ca

Education
- Currently enrolled as a Grade 11 student at Pleasant Secondary School.

Skills
- Successfully completed CPR training with St. John Ambulance.

You may also use this letterhead on your cover letter and list of references. It will give your application a professional look and ensure that each page identifies you.

OBJECTIVE

What is your goal, or objective, with this resumé? Include it. Be as specific as you can about the nature of the work you are seeking—for example, you want to "obtain a summer position in a retail setting."

SKILLS

A skill is something you have learned to do. Think of the skills you have that are relevant to your objective. What positions have you held, for example, as a volunteer or member of a team? What skills did you use in those situations? These do not have to be "big" things—they could include babysitting jobs or helping a neighbour.

Tip: Always include any other language you know, such as French or Arabic, on your resumé. Knowing another language is a valuable skill--and an asset in multicultural Canada.

ACCOMPLISHMENTS

You should list your accomplishments and any employment or volunteer experience on your resumé. If you have won any awards, list those as well. Your

Starting with the fields of work and occupations you have identified with Tool 2, create a plan for improving your resumé and cover letters.

115

CPR training with a reputable organization such as St. John Ambulance is a skill that many employers would want to know about. Include it on your resumé!

accomplishments should be listed in reverse chronological order, meaning that you start the list with your most recent activity and move backward.

Usually, it's important to let an employer know that you handle responsibility well. Don't panic if your experience seems unrelated to the job you're applying for. Remember to think about the transferable skills you have learned that relate to the work you will be doing.

Remember that it's not enough to say you "played on a team" or "volunteered." You should give all the details you can, including names, when these activities occurred, and what you actually did.

DO THE SEARCH

Turbo Resumé Language

Your resumé language must also impress. How would you describe your babysitting job? Would you say, "I looked after kids"? Those words don't exactly showcase your skills. You can search for better language on CareerMATTERS. Notice how "supervised and cared for children" sounds better than "looked after kids."

Here are a few other examples of turbo resumé language:

- "organized activities such as games and outings to provide amusement and exercise"
- "instructed children in personal hygiene and social development"

See how the action verbs used at the beginning of each line are powerful tools that can help you showcase your skills and create an effective resumé.

Wise Words

"Try to recall good things that managers … have said about you. As long as they really said it, you can use these indirect quotes on your resumé. [For example:] Cited by supervisor for problem-solving skills and ability to train staff."

—*Resumé Templates.org*

REFERENCES

References are the people who will vouch for your experience and say favourable things about you. Remember: they should be able to talk about the qualities that the person reading your resumé wants to know you have. These qualities might include being a team player, or being polite, punctual, and dependable.

List your references and their contact information (address, phone number, and email address) on a sheet separate from your resumé. Your references should not include family members or close friends. Consider using past employers, supervisors, teachers, coaches, and community leaders. On your resumé, write: "References available upon request" or "References available at the time of interview." Then be prepared to bring your references sheet with you if you get an interview.

RESUMÉ TYPES

There is no single correct way to format a resumé, but there are three basic types: Chronological, Functional, and Combined. Think about the job and your experience and pick the type that works best for you.

Chronological Resumé

- lists each position the person has held at the top of the resumé
- lists the duties and skills associated with each position
- good format for people with a long work history related to the position they are applying for

Functional Resumé

- highlights the person's skills and how they were acquired at the top of the resumé
- lists work history next
- good format for people who don't have a lot of work experience, or whose work experience is not clearly related to the position they're applying for

Combined Resumé

- lists some key skills at the top of the resumé
- provides a more detailed work history than the functional resumé
- good format for people who have a variety of related and unrelated experience for the position they're applying for

GO SMART ... Resumé Analysis

Your teacher will distribute three resumés created by Katie, Mia, and André. Answer the following questions:

1. Identify each resumé type.
2. What do you notice about the way work experience is listed?
3. What do all three resumés have in common?
4. Which resumé type might be right for you? Why?

1. THINK ABOUT ALL THE ACTIVITIES THAT YOU HAVE BEEN INVOLVED WITH INSIDE AND OUTSIDE OF SCHOOL AND WRITE THEM DOWN.

2. HOW CAN THESE ACTIVITIES, OR THE SKILLS YOU DEVELOPED DOING THEM, HELP YOU IN A PART-TIME OR SUMMER JOB?

Want Ads: What Do They Really Want?

By now you've read about the nine essential skills that employers are seeking (Chapters 2 and 11) and how to package your resumé to put your best foot forward. But have you ever read a want ad and wondered what the employer was *really* looking for?

Read the two want ads below. Each ad contains important information about the skills you would need for that job. Notice, however, that the employer might not refer to any essential skills by name. It's your job to tease out that information.

Retail Salespeople Wanted

The Shoe Box, a national chain of family shoe stores, is opening new locations in Kingston, Thunder Bay, and Sudbury. Dynamic, outgoing salespeople are needed for our team. Salespeople are responsible for assisting customers, fitting shoes, stocking shelves, taking inventory, and working a cash register. Some retail experience is an asset.

Applicants should forward their resumé to:

Personnel Manager, The Shoe Box, Corporate Head Office, 933 Division Street, Ottawa, Ontario K1V 6X0.

Camp Michigama is looking for counsellors!

Are you:

- enthusiastic?
- a leader?
- certified in First Aid and CPR?
- someone who enjoys working with children?
- someone who loves the outdoors?

Then this is the job for you!

Camp Michigama, on the shores of Silver Lake, is a sleepover camp for children ages 7 to 13. Camp counsellors are required to supervise and mentor campers, organize activities with camp staff, and teach sports, horseback riding, crafts, and drama. Camp sessions are two weeks in length and counsellors are expected to work a minimum of two sessions.

For more information, and to apply, contact:

Director, Camp Michigama
P.O. Box 123
Perth, Ontario
K7H 3A0

GO SMART ... Improving Your Resumé

1. Your job is to create a resumé or revise an old one. Use the sample resumés distributed by your teacher (Go Smart, page 117) as a model. Before you begin, find a want ad or think of the job you would like to use the resumé for and write down the essential skills you have that are needed for the job. Include your
   - personal information
   - education
   - objective
   - skills
   - accomplishments
   - a separate page on which you list three references

2. Reread the want ads on page 119—remember to read between the lines. Make a T-chart of the employer's requirements and the essential skill each one represents.

Employer's Requirements	Essential Skills
Employee will be responsible for working a cash register.	Numeracy

Your Cover Letter

Your cover letter tells the employer what position you are applying for, and gives you a chance to tell them a little more about yourself than what is in your resumé. It should be created last, after you are sure what position you are applying for.

GOOD OPENINGS

Remember: your cover letter is your first chance to impress a potential employer. Make sure your opening paragraph grabs and keeps the reader's attention. Refer specifically to the position you are applying for (because many organizations have multiple positions available at any one time).

Here are six ways to open a great cover letter. Keep in mind that "The Safe Bet" is the industry standard; anything else is a calculated risk. How much of a risk are you willing to take?

1. The Safe Bet

I am writing in response to your ad in Saturday's *Free Press* regarding the position of sales associate at Top Dog Pet Supplies.

2. The Name Drop

Your store manager, Diane Solomon, suggested I apply for the sales associate position at Top Dog Pet Supplies.

3. Show Off Your Research

Top Dog Pet Supplies has been Acton's #1 pet supply retailer for the past four years running. I am eager to be part of your dynamic sales team, either at the Acton location or at your newly opened Rockwood store.

4. The Question

What child doesn't dream of having a dog? As a sales associate for Top Dog Pet Supplies, I will help customers select products to enhance the pet ownership experience.

5. Quotable Quotes

As Charlotte Gray once said, "A dog desires affection more than its dinner. Well—almost." As a dog lover with sales experience, I am eager to work for Top Dog Pet Supplies as a sales associate.

6. Flattery Will Get You Everywhere

Every time I enter Top Dog Pet Supplies, I am amazed at the great selection of pet products and at the friendly, knowledgeable staff. I have wanted to be part of your team for some time now, and it was with great excitement that I read your want ad in Saturday's *Free Press* for a sales associate.

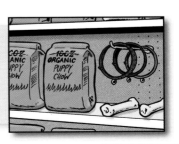

THE BODY PARAGRAPHS

Now that you have the reader's attention, it's time to show them your stuff. Remember that they will read your resumé (if your cover letter is impressive enough), so don't waste time rewriting what's already in your resumé. Use the cover letter as an opportunity to pick two or three key skills from the want ad and tell **anecdotes** to demonstrate that you have those skills.

anecdote
short account of an interesting incident

Be a STAR

When you tell an anecdote in your cover letter, keep in mind the acronym STAR. It works like this:

STory

Action

Result

- Explain the **story** or background of the situation. What was the problem? What needed changing?
- Explain the **action** that you took to resolve the problem or improve the situation.
- Describe the positive **result**, or outcome. Be sure to highlight any transferable skills.

Don't panic if you have no related employment experience (see Career Coach, page 118); the focus is on highlighting the skills that you have that the employer needs.

Skills you need	Skills I have

Using the headings "Skills you need" and "Skills I have," choose three to five key job skills and give proof that you have each skill.

Use a T-Chart

If you are less comfortable with writing paragraphs about yourself, consider using a T-chart instead of the body paragraphs of your cover letter.

THE CLOSER

End your cover letter with a request for action: "I look forward to hearing from you to further discuss my suitability for this position."

GO SMART ... Cover Letters

1. Your teacher will distribute a sample formatted cover letter. Using that example and the information on pages 120–122, think of a job you'd like to apply for and draft your own cover letter.

2. When you have finished your cover letter, reflect on the following questions:

   a) What type of opening did you choose? Why?

   b) What skills did you elaborate on with anecdotes? Do your anecdotes show how you noticed a problem and found a solution (STAR)?

   c) What have you learned about cover letter writing through this exercise?

Completing an Application Form

Many employers will require you to complete an application form in addition to submitting a cover letter and resumé. Some will want you to fill the form out in front of them (a tricky way to test your literacy skills!), so be sure to bring all the tools and information you might need with you, including a blue or black pen, and the names, addresses, phone numbers, and dates of your previous employers, volunteer organizations, and educational institutions.

Your application is part of your first impression—so you don't want to be seen asking for a pen or the Internet in order to complete yours!

Applying for a job at a bookstore ...

GO SMART TOP TEN

APPLICATION FORM BLUNDERS

10. **NOT READING THE INSTRUCTIONS AND FOLLOWING DIRECTIONS**

9. **SPELLING MISTAKES**

8. **NOT PRINTING, MESSY WRITING, CROSSED-OUT WORDS, CRUMPLED PAPER**

7. **NOT APPLYING FOR A SPECIFIC POSITION**

6. **NOT BEING SPECIFIC ABOUT YOUR AVAILABILITY, OR BEING INFLEXIBLE ABOUT WORK HOURS**

5. **BLANK SPACES (IF THERE IS NO ANSWER, PUT N.A. OR "NOT APPLICABLE")**

4. **USE OF WORDS SUCH AS "FIRED" OR "QUIT" WHEN ASKED FOR THE REASON YOU LEFT YOUR LAST JOB (TRY "RETURNED TO SCHOOL," "SEASONAL," OR "CAREER CHANGE" AS MORE POSITIVE OPTIONS)**

3. **FORGETTING TO SIGN YOUR APPLICATION**

2. **MISSING THE DEADLINE TO HAND IN YOUR APPLICATION**

1. **BEING RUDE OR UNPROFESSIONAL TO THE PERSON WHO GIVES YOU THE APPLICATION FORM (THEIR FIRST IMPRESSION OF YOU IS OFTEN PASSED ON)**

Wise Words

"I have always advised people never to apply for a job you do not really want."

—*Michael Todd, American film producer*

ENERGY ◯ ◯ ◯ ◯ ◯

AGE ① ⑥ ◯ ◯ ◯

REAL-TIME RESUMÉ

HELP! What are my rights?

Valerie is busy completing an application form to work as a day camp counsellor this summer. The application asks her if she is over 18, and if she is not, to list her age. Valerie will be 16 in June, and worries that the employer might not hire her in favour of other, older applicants. Her sister tells her that she should leave that question blank, because questions on application forms about age are illegal.

YOU BE THE COACH

How should Valerie answer the question? Give Valerie your best reality check using the tips below. Email or videotape your advice. Then compare your reality check to the one provided by your teacher.

REALITY CHECK

○ The Ontario *Human Rights Code* does not allow employers to ask questions about race, ancestry, place of origin, colour, ethnic origin, citizenship, creed, sex, sexual orientation, age, record of offences, marital status, same-sex partnership status, family status, or handicap.

○ Employers can ask if it is legal for a candidate to work in Canada, or if the candidate has the necessary skills needed to perform the job (such as fluency in English for a receptionist's position).

○ Although employers can't ask for your date of birth, they are allowed to ask if you are over 18 years of age. Many jobs have a legal minimum age requirement, and in those cases, employers must make sure the applicant meets the legal age requirement.

 Read the Summary on page 125. Are there any ideas you are unsure of? Are there any skills you need to practise? If so, go back and review them.

This chapter introduced you to the following ideas:

1. When applying for a job, your resumé is what makes the first impression: make sure that yours is polished.

2. Your resumé shows what you have done: what level of education you have, personal accomplishments such as first aid certification, and job and volunteer experience.

3. References are an important part of applying for a job. Choose past employers, teachers, and contacts (not friends or family) who can discuss your qualities.

4. Figure out from job ads exactly what skills the employer is looking for. Employers need to see that you have the qualities and skills they seek.

5. Cover letters introduce your resumé and yourself to a potential employer. Follow the paragraph model and your own approach (pages 120–122) to engage, inform, and impress.

6. Many employers require you to complete an application form (sometimes on the spot). Be prepared with everything you will need: pens, and all relevant information.

7. When applying for a job, you need to impress your potential employer: following instructions, not making spelling mistakes, printing neatly, and showing flexibility and politeness are key.

Confident that you are ready to move forward?
Then go to the next chapter.

125

Bombing at the Interview

Louise thought she was going to have it made: "I was so excited to get the interview at the Camera Shack. I figured I had the job locked up; I have been taking 35mm and digital photos since I was a kid and I volunteer at the local community centre teaching photography to seniors."

Despite her great qualifications, Louise did not get the job.

"I guess I wasn't all that shocked," she says. "I had a terrible interview! I walked into the interview room and there were four people on one side of a big table. Totally intimidating! They asked me all these questions about the company and what my plan was for the job—stuff I hadn't even thought about, let alone researched.

"I was so mad at myself afterwards. If I hadn't been so overconfident, I would have spent way more time preparing for the interview. I won't make that mistake again!"

Louise was confident going into the interview. She knows a lot about cameras and photography.

DO THE SEARCH

- How was Louise unprepared for her interview?
- How could you research a company to prepare for your interview? Why would this be important?
- How might being interviewed by a panel of people differ from being interviewed by one person?
- Why is it important to have a plan or goal for your work at a particular job?

Wise Words

"I was going into the interview and the sole of my shoe fell off. I took it in stride. In fact, the humour this incident produced created an instant good rapport between the interviewer and myself."

—*Lyse Verlez, student and would-be movie reviewer*

Review your passions, preferences, and smarts from Tool 1.
Is there anything else to add?

Interview Basics: What to Expect

No matter what the job, interviews generally follow a basic structure. Knowing what to expect will not only help you prepare your answers—it will go a long way toward relieving your anxiety.

1. Introductions

The interviewer(s) and you will introduce yourselves, usually with a handshake.

2. Small Talk

Don't be surprised if the first couple of questions are about the weather, or if you'd like a glass of water—interviewers usually start with a little small talk to help you settle your nerves and make you feel more comfortable.

3. General Questions

Here's where the interview really starts; you might be asked what you know about the company, or how you heard about the job. This is where you can show off your research or your connections to people in the company (networking).

DO THE SEARCH

4. Skills and Experience Questions

This is when the interviewer asks you about your skills that relate to the job. Remember to always provide proof of your skills, by explaining a situation in which you used or improved that skill. Use the STAR method described in Chapter 9 (page 122) to structure your answers.

5. Strengths and Weaknesses

This is a very popular type of interview question. Most people are good at describing a strength, such as the most central skill for the job, or an important skill not yet discussed, but it can be hard to talk about weaknesses. Will they still want to hire you if you confess to being less than perfect? Of course they will—if you practise how to answer this question!

There are a few key things to remember about the weakness question:

- ✘ Never choose something central to the job (for example, don't say that kids make you nervous if you are applying to work at a day camp).
- ✘ Never give more than one weakness.
- ✘ Never discuss a weakness that you aren't doing anything to improve.

You can really use this last point to your advantage. Turn the frown upside down by discussing a weakness and also explaining how you are working to fix it—this not only covers the question but also shows the interviewer that you are self-aware and always trying to improve yourself!

Starting with the fields of work and occupations you have identified with Tool 2, create a plan for improving your interview skills.

The Sandwich Formula

Here's a formula to try: start and finish with a positive statement and put the weakness in the middle. Here's how it works:

➕ "I know how important it is not to spend too much time on an assigned task." (the positive)

➖ "Sometimes my need to strive for perfection slows me down." (the weakness)

➕ "I've found it helpful to check with my supervisor to see if I really need to spend more time on the task." (actions to improve)

6. Deep Thoughts

Sometimes interviewers will ask you stress questions (see the section on page 133) or questions on your future goals and aspirations. Don't let these more unconventional questions rattle you, and never panic if you need a little time to think about your answer. Interviewers generally use these types of questions to find out more about your values and personality, to see if you are a good fit for the organization and the people you'll be working with.

7. Any Questions?

This is the point in the interview where you will be asked if you have any questions for the interviewer. This is a good time to show off your research and interest in the organization by asking about future plans, training opportunities, or how you can prepare for the job. As a general rule, avoid asking about salary, **benefits**, and time off at this point. Sometimes, though, the interviewer may ask you about salary, so it is a good idea to research a typical wage for someone with your experience and qualifications and to think about what salary you expect, just in case it comes up.

DO THE SEARCH

benefits
services provided by an employer in addition to wages, such as life insurance or drug and dental plans

GO SMART ... Researching Interview Questions in Advance

1. You can prepare for interview questions by making a skills T-chart. Using the headings "Skills They Want" and "Examples and Anecdotes," come up with one or two examples of how you demonstrate each skill. Think about some recent situations in which you used that skill or explain how you dealt with a particular problem by using the skill.

2. On your computer or in your notebook, begin a file of possible interview questions.

   a) Review this chapter and note some of the typical interview questions. You could also type "interview questions" into a search engine. There are thousands of websites that list typical (and unusual) interview questions. Add some of these questions to your file.

   DO THE SEARCH

   b) Type out your answers and save them to review each time you prepare for an interview.

   c) As you go to job interviews, add those questions to your file. If you get feedback from the interviewer, consider using this advice to improve your answers for next time.

   Remember: the purpose of this file is to help you recall and organize your experience, *not* to create a series of answers that you will memorize. If you memorize answers, you might not answer the question exactly and your delivery might be rushed or robotic.

1. COMPARE JOHN'S APPEARANCE BEFORE AND AFTER THE MAKE-OVER. WHAT FACTORS HELPED JOHN GET THE JOB INTERVIEW?

2. MAKE A PLAN TO ENSURE THAT A POTENTIAL EMPLOYER GETS A POSITIVE FIRST IMPRESSION OF YOU. THINK ABOUT YOUR CLOTHES, GROOMING, AND WHAT YOU WILL NEED TO BRING WITH YOU FOR YOUR JOB SEARCH.

3. COMPOSE A FASHION LIST OF DON'TS FOR MAKING A GOOD FIRST IMPRESSION IN A JOB INTERVIEW.

Making Body Language Work for You

Knowing about body language is the first step toward making it work for you. Body language is talk with your body. It includes the way you are standing or sitting; the gestures you make with your hands or arms; and the expression on your face.

Effective body language works for you. It complements (works with) what you are saying to communicate a total message. Ineffective body language can be confusing (your mouth says one thing and your gestures say another) or hostile (you look scary). It can cause people to stop listening altogether.

Have you ever watched a politician deliver a speech to the public? Don't think for a second that he or she hasn't practised the body language as much as the words! The following are some of the best body language tricks for your interview.

THE HANDSHAKE

The first thing you will do at your interview is greet the interviewer with a handshake; it is also how you generally end your interview. First and last impressions are lasting, so why not practise an effective handshake? You don't want to be the one whose handshake is too limp (makes you look wimpy) or too firm (makes you look too competitive or even cruel).

Reach forward with your right arm until the web of your hand (the soft part between your thumb and pointer finger) meets the web of the other person's hand. Clasp hands (like a squeeze) firmly but not too hard, and shake once or twice only. Release the hand (not too quickly, as if you hated touching them, but don't hold on so long it gets uncomfortable). The reason you need to practise this is that you must do the whole handshake while maintaining eye contact, smiling, and speaking (introducing yourself or thanking the interviewer)!

Always follow your interviewer's lead on this one; some people may choose not to shake hands for religious reasons, but they will usually cross their arms over their chest to indicate this. Don't act embarrassed if you've extended your arm; just continue with your greeting as you move your arm back to your side.

Think you could make the ultimate video on the ultimate handshake? See Go Smart, page 132.

YOU BE THE COACH

When Tosh met his interviewer, he shook hands quickly and mumbled his name, looking down at the floor. Coach Tosh in better body language for this situation.

OPEN POSTURE

Good posture is always important (slouching makes you look lazy), but open posture makes you look honest, and interested in sharing. Practise open posture by sitting on the edge of your chair, leaning ever so slightly forward. Don't cross your legs or arms—believe it or not, crossing makes you look like you want to keep things to yourself, or that you're hiding something. Put your hands on top of your thighs, palms up.

> **YOU BE THE COACH**
>
> Annalee flopped down onto her chair and crossed her legs. She was cold, so she kept her hands balled into fists at her interview. Coach Annalee in better body language for this situation.

GESTURES

Don't overdo this aspect of body language. Too many hand movements are very distracting, and can even make you look ridiculous. Small movements of your hands can do a lot to emphasize your points, and show your interest.

> **YOU BE THE COACH**
>
> Allan's friends tell him he moves his hands too much when he speaks, so he decides to sit on his hands at his job interview. Coach Allan in better body language for this situation.

EYE CONTACT

This is the most crucial part of positive body language. Eye contact shows your interviewer that you are honest, and really interested in what you are telling them. It can be tough to look people in the eyes, especially if you're nervous, so practise this skill with a partner.

> **YOU BE THE COACH**
>
> Leila doesn't know what to do—her mother has always taught her not to look at adults in the eyes, as a sign of respect, but her father insists that Canadians expect eye contact when two people are speaking to each other, regardless of age. Leila has a job interview tomorrow. Coach her in appropriate body language for this situation.

Good eye contact goes a long way to making a good first impression.

NERVES

Everyone has different **physiological** signs of nervousness. Your body produces **adrenaline** to help you keep alert in stressful situations, and that can often result in physical **symptoms** of stress. Some people get headaches or butterflies in their stomachs, but sometimes symptoms of stress are more obvious. Maybe you tend to get red in the face, or a dry mouth, or sweaty hands (or underarms!), or even a facial twitch.

> **YOU BE THE COACH**
>
> Tristan hates it, but whenever he speaks in public, he goes completely red. He is certain that his interviewer will know how nervous he is, and Tristan wants to look more confident. Coach Tristan in better body language for this situation.

If you are worried about sweat and body odour, make sure that you arrive at your interview freshly showered and dressed. Try to avoid rushing to the location. And whatever you do, don't go overboard on perfume or cologne; some people are allergic to fragrances.

The important thing to remember is that no matter how much you prepare for an interview, you will still be a little nervous, and you can't do much about how your body handles stress. Interviewers understand that people get nervous, and they will try to set you at ease as much as they can. Your expression (smile!) and sincerity will go a long way to make up for any nervous habits.

physiological
referring to an organism's (in this case, a person's) normal or typical functioning

adrenaline
hormone secreted by the body to help it deal with physical or emotional stress

symptom
sign or indication of something

GO SMART ... Body Language

1. With a partner, role-play one of the following job interview situations using effective body language. Tape yourself or have another student observe and make notes on your performance. Be sure to consider all of the points on pages 127–131. Get feedback and then switch roles.

   a) You are applying to a camp counsellor's job. There are two interviewers: the owner of the camp and the head counsellor. They ask you all the typical questions but also ask you a scenario question: "How would you handle a situation where one camper in your cabin is being teased and excluded by all his cabin mates?"

   b) You are applying to work as a tour guide. There is one interviewer who asks the typical questions but also asks you to role-play a "guided tour" of your home.

   c) You are applying to volunteer at a senior's residence. There is a panel interviewing you, including the head nurse, the activities coordinator, and the volunteer coordinator. They each ask you two of the typical questions. At the end of the interview, they ask you if you have questions for any of them.

   d) You are interviewing for a co-op placement at an auto body shop. The manager is asking you all the typical questions but he also wants to know why you are interested in the co-op program and in his shop in particular.

   e) You are applying to work at a fast-food restaurant. Your interviewers are the owner and the manager, who ask you all the typical questions. The owner also asks you if you think that her restaurant is better or worse than the competition and why.

   f) You are applying to work as a summer student in a large company. You are interviewed by a human resources manager and by the supervisor of your department (this could be reception, manufacturing, or customer service). They ask you all the typical questions but also ask you what your plans are when the summer is over.

   g) You are applying to work at a retail clothing store. The manager is interviewing you and asks you all the typical questions. Toward the end of the interview, she says, "I'm still not convinced that you are right for our team—I have interviewed other candidates, who all have more retail experience than you."

2. In small groups, create your own one- or two-minute handshake instructional video (or skit) using the handshake guidelines on page 130. Decide on an audience for your video (peers, adults, younger students). Include some do's and don'ts. You'll need a narrator and a few models. Share your video with your classmates.

Wise Words

"Whatever you do, do not fall asleep during your interview."

—*Radio show on interview techniques*

Waiting for an interview is nerve-wracking. Relax. You already made it to the interview. Now they need to see the real you and whether they could work with you.

Testing Your Stress Q

One strategy for interviewers is to ask an unexpected or **unconventional** question to see not only what you'll say, but also how you'll manage the stress of the situation. It sounds mean, but stress questions give interviewers a lot of valuable information. Can you think on the spot? Do you listen very carefully to how the question is worded? Will you react with grace under pressure?

But don't get too stressed out—the good news is that you can prepare for stress questions, just as you would any other interview questions. Stress questions usually fall into three main categories.

 ## THE SCENARIO

This is the most common stress question. The interviewer will ask you to imagine that you are in a certain type of situation and ask you how you would deal with that situation. Your job is to demonstrate good problem-solving skills and an understanding of your role and responsibilities. How can you prepare for a scenario question? Think of the types of situations you might encounter at work, and how a good employee would deal with them.

 ## WHAT'S YOUR FAVOURITE ... ?

This type of stress question is becoming quite popular, because your answer can reveal quite a lot about your values. The interviewer will ask you about your favourite author, or colour, or animal, or about the most recent movie you've seen or book you've read.

You can prepare for this question by reviewing your skills and the values you think are relevant to the job, and then by brainstorming a number of things that tie into that. Always try to relate those unconventional questions back to the job that you are applying for. This shows creativity and will earn you interview bonus points!

If the most recent movie you've seen or book you've read doesn't have a great theme for your purposes, simply choose the movie or book that best fits the value you want to demonstrate. For example, you could say, "Just the other day, I saw *Star Wars* again. I have always admired Luke Skywalker's beliefs and his loyalty to his friends—he is a true hero. I think that children today need positive role models in their lives. This is why I want to be a camp counsellor."

 ## THE PUT-DOWN

This is the toughest stress question, and requires you to listen carefully and not lose your cool. The interviewer might say something like, "I'm still not convinced that you are the right person for the job," or "What would you say if I told you this was a terrible interview?" First, don't get angry or defensive! Calmly and politely express regret—for example, "I am sorry you feel that way"—and then go on to emphasize your strongest skills or qualifications.

The best way to prepare for the put-down question is to review your skills and qualifications, and to remember that, at most interviews, the questions are prepared ahead of time for all candidates—it's not personal!

unconventional
out of the ordinary

Interview going badly? Don't panic. Be pleasant. End on a good note (if possible). There is always a next time.

If you want to show your eco-friendliness, you might compare yourself to the colour green because "it's the colour of nature and I love the natural world."

REAL-TIME RESUMÉ

How do I answer that?

Grant is excited to have his first interview for a job at a local sporting goods store. His interview is going pretty well until the store manager asks, "Describe a book you've read recently that you really enjoyed." Grant panics, because although he loves sports, his favourite books are all fantasy. He hasn't a clue how this question relates at all to the job he's interviewing for.

SPORTS ◯ ◯ ◯ ◯ ◯

FANTASY ◯ ◯ ◯ ◯ ◯

ANSWERS ❓ ❓ ❓ ● ●

Wise Words

"Never wear a backward baseball cap to an interview unless applying for the job of umpire."
—Dan Zevin, author

YOU BE THE COACH

How should Grant answer this question? Give Grant your best reality check using the tips below. Role-play with a partner and show how you would answer the store manager's question. Explain what aspect of your personality is revealed in your answer.

Bonus round: The store manager's next question is, "If you were an animal, what would you be?" Show how you would answer that and explain why. Then compare your advice to the advice provided by your teacher.

REALITY CHECK

- Even if it seems weird or unrelated to the job, *every* question in an interview is important and reveals your personality. Employers use these types of interview questions to learn more about what you're like—your values.

- Pausing to think of a good answer is totally acceptable. It's worse to panic and blurt out the wrong thing.

- Explaining the "why" of an answer helps interviewers get to know you and your values. Connecting a response to the job itself is even better.

 Read the Summary on page 135. Are there any ideas you are unsure of? Are there any skills you need to practise? If so, go back and review them.

Believe in yourself, and the interviewer will too! Remember that just getting to the interview stage is a huge accomplishment. They know you're qualified, so the interview is all about you and the interviewer getting a sense whether you are a good fit for each other. Be proud of your achievements, and be yourself.

This chapter introduced you to the following ideas:

1. Don't go to an interview unprepared! Take the time to research the company and the position. Think about what your goals are for working at this job.

2. There is a pattern to most interviews. Get familiar with it. Role-play being at an interview with friends or family. Turn those routine questions to your advantage!

3. The strengths-and-weaknesses question is a favourite among interviewers. Be sure to answer with only one minor weakness, and something you are working on. Try the sandwich formula (page 128).

4. How you present yourself (even before the interview) is key. Dress nicely to drop off your application or resumé. Smile, shake hands, and make a good first impression!

5. Body language can make or break an interview. It starts with the handshake. Practise a friendly, relaxed handshake. Work on your body language so that it doesn't work against you!

6. Stress is a big factor at interviews. Know yourself and how you react in stressful situations (panel interviews are a killer!). Be ready to calmly answer difficult questions.

7. The best way to sell yourself at an interview is to prepare: dress well, practise how to answer questions, research the company, believe in yourself … and, above all, arrive on time!

Confident that you are ready to move forward?
Then go to the next chapter.

135

Smart Success at Work

What's My Job?

So you think you can identify a person's occupation by the clothes he or she wears? Let's test that idea.

We sent a photographer to take pictures of people in downtown Toronto on a business day. Can you identify each person's occupation? What do the clothes tell you about each person?

- How did you do?
- Based on this exercise, what can you say about the first impressions people make on others?
- How will you use this information in your future job searches?

Review your passions, preferences, and smarts from Tool 1.
Is there anything else to add?

First Impressions Count

A first impression is an opinion reached about a person almost instantaneously. First impressions are crucial in the world of work. Researchers suggest that it takes only one-tenth of a second for us to make up our minds about people. Always try to create the best first impression you can. Even if you are nervous, a warm smile and a firm handshake will help—and it will help set you at ease too. (See the tips on handshakes on page 130.)

How is a first impression formed?

55%	By how you *look*—your dress, facial expression, body language
38%	By your *tone* of voice
7%	By *what* you actually say

How can you use the information in this table to help when you apply for a job?

Top Ten Ways to Make a Good First Impression at Work

- Have a positive attitude.
- Dress professionally (blend with co-workers).
- Learn co-workers' names quickly.
- Ask questions and ask for help.
- Take notes about important information.
- Learn as much as you can about the company.
- Avoid rumours and gossip.
- Listen more than you talk.
- Keep your boss informed.
- Show appreciation to people who help you.

GO SMART ... Good First Impressions

Using the Top Ten Ways to Make a Good First Impression at Work, provide a specific example for five of the points given. Make your examples specific to you and a situation you have encountered in applying for a part-time job or volunteer position, or at school. Example: "I thanked our guidance counsellor when he showed me options for how to pay for college."

Starting with the fields of work and occupations you have identified with Tool 2, envision your first day on the job. Use this chapter as a checklist of things to know and do.

137

First Day on the Job

The big day has arrived. It's 7 a.m. and you have a job to go to.

Getting off to a great start on the job involves a little planning ahead of time. Here are some tips for ensuring that your first day goes smoothly.

THE FIRST DAY GAME PLAN

ARRIVAL Do you know your start and finish times, the address of the work location, and how to get there? Take a map with you in case you get lost. Ask if you need to bring anything with you. (Some jobs require you to bring identification.) Be sure you have all the workplace contact information with you in case you or a family member needs it.

employee training session
period of time devoted to training employees for specific aspects of their job

employee manual
company handbook that explains a company's policies and practices with respect to employees—e.g., dress code, office behaviour, and Internet access

ORIENTATION Whom should you ask for when you arrive? What is the name of your supervisor? Find out if you will be taking any special training, such as safety training. Ask about an **employee training session** or **manual**. Ask where the washrooms are! And don't forget to ask how long you have for breaks and lunch.

EXPECTATIONS Ask about any information you should have about the job or the company in order to do the job well. Do you require a uniform? Is there a dress code? Ask about any rules or routines that you are expected to follow. Visit the company website beforehand to gather important information such as company history, goals, and products or services they provide.

RESPONSIBILITIES What tasks will you have to perform? Should you get started or wait for instructions? Who will give you instructions or assistance? Do you have deadlines? What are they? Are you supposed to wait for someone to take over your work when it is time to leave?

Many teen workers must wear a uniform at their job. They are expected to wear the uniform with pride, because they are representing the company to the public.

GO SMART ... First Day on the Job

DO THE SEARCH Go to the Canada's Wonderland website and click on Jobs. Using the information in the First Day Game Plan as a guide, create a chart that gathers the important information you would need for your first day on the job.

Essential Skills in Action

In Chapter 2, you learned about the **essential skills** needed for school, work, and life. These skills are essential because they are the basis for all learning and enable you to adapt to situations in the workplace.

essential skills
skills that are essential because they are the basis of all other skills

The Essential Skills

Reading	Understanding materials written in sentences or paragraphs (e.g., letters, manuals)
Document Use	Using and understanding labels, graphs, signs, and other similar materials
Numeracy	Using and understanding numbers
Writing	Writing text or typing on a computer
Oral Communication	Using speech to share thoughts and information
Working with Others	Interacting with others to complete tasks
Thinking	Reviewing information to make decisions
Computer Use	Using computers and other technical tools
Continuous Learning	Participating in an ongoing process of gaining skills and knowledge (e.g., workplace training)

GO SMART ... Essential Skills

DO THE SEARCH

Web Activity: Assessing Your Essential Skills
- Go to Human Resources and Skills Development Canada's Essential Skills website.
- Complete the Essential Skills Toolkit Indicators online and find out more about your essential skills.

REAL-TIME RESUMÉ

Expert Level

INTRODUCTION

You have been hired to help the people in one of these situations. Read each scenario and make your selection.

SCENARIO 1: Messy Home for Sale

YOUR JOB: Real Estate Agent

The Rathers are selling their home and want you to be their real estate agent. However, they say they don't have time to make any repairs or clean up the mess. Fifteen-year-old daughter Mara doesn't want to move at all and locks her bedroom door when you visit. The Rathers have a large home that will fetch a good price—provided that everyone gets on board with your plan. Use the line master distributed by your teacher to coach the Rathers and solve this problem.

SCENARIO 2: Executive Can't Communicate

YOUR JOB: Communication Coach

Spiffy Corp. has a great new product geared to high school students. The SmartAgenda comes with a log-on homework feature that lets you get online homework assistance in key subject areas. The more agenda accessories you buy, the more online assistance you get. However, Spiffy's product consultant, Dave, can't give a convincing product presentation. When he practised on his own team, he achieved the results shown here. You've just been hired as a communication coach to help Spiffy Corp. fix this problem. Use the line master distributed by your teacher.

SCENARIO 3: Unsafe Auto Body Shop

YOUR JOB: Safety Inspector

Alfred and Elena Varga are car collectors with their own auto body shop. Currently, they are looking for apprentice mechanics. However, their son has told them that the shop has some safety issues, such as poor ventilation, slippery surfaces, and incorrect disposal of hazardous waste, which should be addressed first. You are a retired safety inspector who has agreed to look at the Vargas' shop. Use the line master distributed by your teacher to document your findings, coach the Vargas, and solve this problem.

DO THE SEARCH ▶

> **REALITY CHECK** During this process, you will be using many essential skills such as writing, numeracy, thinking, and communication to identify the problem, arrive at a solution, and communicate with the people you are working for. To help you decide which scenario you would like to choose, research each occupation first on Career Cruising. Then use the handouts provided by your teacher.

The Smarts Nobody Talks About

On the job, you need different kinds of smarts. The essential skills represent one kind. However, there are other skills that you may need in different situations.

NEGOTIATION SKILLS

Negotiation is a method of problem solving. It is done when two people want something but can't agree on what it should be. For example, you may encounter a situation in which you need a day off work for an important event. In this case, you will need to negotiate with your boss about how to make up the time if you are to be paid for that day. Negotiations may also occur between groups of employees and an employer to try to arrive at an agreement on an employment contract.

Steps to Negotiating Anything

Focus on what's important	What do you want or need? What does the other person want or need? Speak and listen carefully.	*Very important!*
Generate ideas	Think of many different options before deciding how to solve the problem.	
Seek alternatives	Not every negotiation results in agreement. What alternatives are there?	
Be fair	Make sure you both get a chance to take part in the discussion.	
Build relationships	Keep the lines of communication strong. Stay respectful (see page 146).	

GO SMART ... Negotiating

Work with a partner to identify the best way to negotiate two of the following situations.

- You wish to spend more time with your friends but a family member would prefer if you spent more time on your homework.
- You need time off work to study for exams but your supervisor wants you to work more hours because it's a busy time of year.
- Your coach needs you to attend a very important practice to prepare for the big game but it is on your best friend's birthday and you already have plans to celebrate with her after school.
- Your teacher has made arrangements for you to write a test on a day you will be away on a school trip.

DIFFICULT CONVERSATIONS IN THE WORKPLACE

A difficult conversation is anything you find hard to talk about. Asking for a raise. Confronting a disrespectful or hurtful comment from a co-worker. Apologizing. Being drawn into a discussion about sexuality, race, or gender.

There are some common themes in these examples:

vulnerable
with your defences down; as though you could be attacked

- You feel **vulnerable**.
- The issues at stake are important and the outcome of the conversation is uncertain.
- You care deeply about what is being discussed.

Think of a difficult conversation you had recently. Try to remember and record who said what, and how the conversation ended. Now, break the conversation down into three parts. What happened? Who is to blame? How did you feel? Now examine each part in more detail.

Difficult conversations crop up everywhere: between friends, at home ... even in the workplace. Knowing strategies to deal with difficult conversations will help you in life—and in any future career.

What happened?

This is really about who's right. Of course, you assume that you are right. So does the other person. That's why these conversations often fail. When you use "right" as your starting point, no one can agree.

▶ What you can do instead

Instead of assuming that you are right, and then trying to prove it, try to see what the other person perceives or values. Instead of delivering a message about how right you are, ask the other person some questions to gain understanding of his or her viewpoint. This will help to cool down the discussion too.

Who's to blame?

Most difficult conversations focus attention on who is to blame for the mess you're in. But talking about blame only produces denial. Also, each side will put a lot of energy into claiming that their side is right.

▶ What you can do instead

Instead of playing the blame game, you can explore why things went wrong and how they might be corrected going forward.

How do I feel?

Difficult conversations are also about emotions or feelings, and many people try to avoid discussing them. Perhaps you want to remain rational. You don't want your judgment clouded by feelings. Bringing up feelings can also be scary and uncomfortable.

▶ What you can do instead

Go ahead and talk about your feelings using I-messages (see page 57). The more practice you get talking about your feelings, the more skilled you will become at it.

Understanding these three questions will help you see that you don't have a "message to deliver," but rather some information to share and some questions to ask. Instead of wanting to persuade and get your way, you can understand what has happened from the other person's point of view, explain your point of view, share and understand feelings, and work together to figure out a way to manage the problem going forward.

GO SMART | ... Difficult Conversations

Identify a difficult conversation you had to have at home, at school, or at work. Write a paragraph to describe how you could have handled things more effectively. Use a chart like this one to list your main points.

Difficult Conversations

What I did	What I could have done differently and will try next time

Managing Mistakes at Work

Everybody makes mistakes. In fact, mistakes are part of the learning process. By making errors you gain understanding and learn how to do things correctly.

It can be embarrassing and even frightening to make a mistake at your job or at school. But sometimes people unwittingly make things worse by avoiding the mistake or by not handling it effectively.

Here's an action plan to deal with mistakes on and off the job.

TOP FIVE WAYS TO MANAGE A MISTAKE

Take the High Road: Admit your Mistake

It's important to show your boss that you are a responsible person who can admit to a mistake. The outcome will be much worse if someone else catches your mistake and reports it. Be sure to jot down the details so that you get all the information to the boss.

Make a Plan to Fix the Problem

It's also important to have a plan for fixing the mistake. Present your plan clearly and be open to suggestions that the boss can provide. You may need to spend some of your own time correcting the mistake.

Use a Problem-Solving Model

A problem-solving model can help you organize your ideas for resolving the mistake and make a good decision. (A problem-solving model will be distributed by your teacher.)

Don't Blame Others for Your Mistake

Own your own mistake. If others are involved, encourage those who share responsibility to follow your lead, and talk to the boss.

Use the Mistake as a Learning Opportunity

Try to make sure you don't make the same mistake twice. Use the mistake as an opportunity to approach the situation or problem differently next time.

Wise Words

"Experience is the name everyone gives to their mistakes."

—Oscar Wilde,
Irish playwright

Don't try to ignore your mistakes. Learn from them!

GO SMART — ... Managing Mistakes

1. In small groups create a funny skit that shows a silly mistake made at work. Show the wrong solution first and then the correct one.

2. Use the Top Five Ways to Manage a Mistake while advising in the following situations. Write out the mistake and your recommendation on how to handle it.

   a) Michel skipped a class to go to the mall with his friends. His teacher has called and left messages at home wanting to speak to his parents.

   b) Fran forgot her textbook in her locker. She needs it for a big assignment that's due tomorrow.

   c) Katie copied some answers on a test from the student sitting next to her and she thinks the teacher saw her doing it.

   d) Raj accidentally broke his friend's MP3 player that he borrowed during lunch.

Character Matters

On the job, character matters as much as it does any place else. In fact, the workplace is a place where your character is tested every day. Brush up on these character challenges and think about how you would like to be perceived at work.

RESPONSIBILITY

When you joined the basketball team, you accepted the responsibility of being a team member. You agreed to go to practices, wear the uniform, be on time for games, and listen to your coach. Responsibility means that people depend on you and want to know they can count on your participation. It means making a commitment and going to practices even when you don't feel like it because you made a promise to help the team.

There are different types of responsibility. They include:

- **Moral responsibility** to other people, animals, and the earth. This means treating other people fairly and being kind to living things, and caring for the environment.

- **Legal responsibility** involves following the laws of your community, province, and country.

- **Family responsibility** means keeping your commitments to your parents or guardians, siblings, and other relatives. This might involve completing things you promised to do around the house. This might also involve taking part in family activities such as attending a religious service.

When you play team sports, you have a responsibility to your teammates—to show up for practices and games, to play as well as you can, and to have the right attitude.

- **Community responsibility** can involve contributions made to your school or neighbourhood that shows commitment to making your local area a better place. This can be demonstrated through donating time to assist a charity, hospital, community centre, or school. A community cleanup is a perfect example!

- **Personal responsibility** is all the actions that you take to show your commitment to other roles and people in your life. You might show your teachers that you are reliable by completing the assigned work on time. You might show responsibility to your parents by completing all your chores at home without being asked.

GO SMART ... Responsibilities in the Workplace

DO THE SEARCH

1. Conduct research online about responsibilities in the workplace. Each of the following laws outlines responsibilities for both the employee and the employer in the workplace. Select five key ideas included in these laws.

   a) *Employment Standards Act*

   b) *Occupational Health and Safety Act*

   c) Ontario *Human Rights Code*

2. Identify three celebrities and research their behaviour in their public or private lives. Write a brief response indicating whether you feel they are showing responsibility in their everyday lives. Do they make good role models for young people?

RESPECT

respect
treating something or someone with consideration and thoughtfulness

Respect involves showing consideration and appreciation for people, their property, and the environment. It involves treating other people the way you would like to be treated, and honouring other people's needs, wants, differences, and beliefs and values.

You can show that you respect a person by giving them your consideration and positive attention, and by being courteous. For example, on the job, you could demonstrate respect by holding the door open for a person trying to get into a room with their hands full, or by welcoming a new employee. You can demonstrate respect for diversity by being willing to accept other people's differences.

Holding the door open for someone is a great example of showing respect. You can hold the door open for an elderly person or for someone who is disabled. At work, you might hold a door open for someone carrying a lot of boxes.

Respect for your environment might involve appreciating the need to show pride in your surroundings. It might involve cleaning up your lunch and not leaving it for others to dispose of. At work, it could mean recycling paper, tin cans, and bottles and respecting the grounds by not littering.

GO SMART ┆ ... Respect at Work

1. Vicky and Safiya work together at a local fast-food restaurant. In fact, Safiya helped to get Vicky hired. Recently, their supervisor has been praising Vicky and criticizing Safiya. He also makes disparaging comments about Safiya's headscarf. Safiya dislikes Mr. Elmer's comments and wants to report to another supervisor. She turns to Vicky for her support.

   - How can Vicky maintain respect and positive relationships with both her friend and her supervisor?
   - What can Vicky do to help Safiya?
   - What values will Vicky demonstrate if she steps forward to assist?

Safiya and Vicky work together at a fast-food restaurant. Safiya is not being treated with respect by her supervisor. What could Vicky do to help her friend and improve the situation?

2. There are many ways that students and members of the school staff can demonstrate respect for the school building, people, and community. In small groups, list things you can do in the places and situations that follow to show respect for your surroundings. Be prepared to share your ideas.

Checklist

○ I can respect school property (classroom, cafeteria, library, lockers, computers) by

_____.

○ I can respect people at school (students, teachers, caretakers, secretaries, administrators) by

_____.

○ I can respect the school environment by

_____.

○ I can respect myself at school by

_____.

HONESTY AND INTEGRITY

Honesty isn't just about being truthful, fair, and genuine with other people—it also means being truthful to yourself. In most cases, it is better to admit your mistakes because covering up for them reveals dishonesty. Employers value employees whom they feel they can trust.

1. WHAT ARE THE ADVANTAGES OF NOT COVERING UP A BAD SITUATION AT SCHOOL OR WORK BY LYING?

2. HAS SOPHIA GAINED THE TRUST OF HER EMPLOYER? WHY OR WHY NOT?

GO SMART ... Honesty Pays Off

1. List some examples of what honesty means to you.

2. Role-play in small groups how to best respond in these situations:

   ● A co-worker tells you he is stealing cash from the gas station where you both work. He is a good friend and he helped you get the job. He asks you to keep the money in your wallet so no one knows he took it. Two weeks later the supervisor asks all employees about the missing money.

   ● You work at a clothing store and get a 5 percent **commission** on your sales. Your manager has encouraged you to do what you need to do to get a sale because it is a slow month for the store. A customer comes into the store and tells you she is going to a job interview and really likes one of the suits in the store window. She tries on the suit but it doesn't fit her that well. She asks, "How do I look?"

3. Find a newspaper article where a business person, politician, celebrity, or public figure has lied about something. What were the consequences that that person faced?

commission
percentage paid to you of the total amount of merchandise you sell

DO THE SEARCH

Initiative and Opportunity: The Yin and Yang of Job Success

Once you have found the right post-secondary placement for you—a job, community involvement **opportunity**, co-operative education placement, or volunteer placement—your next challenge will be to grow on the job. One way you can do that is to show **initiative**.

Showing initiative involves taking action without being prompted by others. Showing initiative in your work will help you to perform well, will get you noticed as an outstanding team member, and may even get you a promotion or more work. It shows that you are eager to do what needs to be done without having to be told to do it. This is why initiative and opportunity are like **yin and yang**.

opportunity
favourable situation or chance to do something

initiative
ability to take action without being prompted by someone else

yin and yang
in Chinese philosophy, two opposing but complementary forces in the universe

Wise Words

"Success usually comes to those who are too busy to be looking for it."
—*Henry David Thoreau, American philosopher*

INITIATIVE

OPPORTUNITY

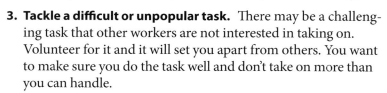

FIVE WAYS TO STAND OUT—AND MAKE THE MOST OF WORK

1. **Find a mentor.** Find someone in your workplace you trust and respect to assist you in getting familiar with the new environment and help you adapt to the new culture.

2. **Get to know the boss.** Take some time to figure out your boss's priorities. Know what his or her goals are and how you can best help achieve those goals.

3. **Tackle a difficult or unpopular task.** There may be a challenging task that other workers are not interested in taking on. Volunteer for it and it will set you apart from others. You want to make sure you do the task well and don't take on more than you can handle.

4. **Show that you are a member of the team.** Take part in or help organize a company event like a work party. This will increase your chances of getting noticed. Your interest in supporting the work community will show you are a team player.

5. **Be proactive about learning.** Keep up to date with the new ideas in the company and take advantage of training opportunities available.

Researching the company your are working for or would like to work for is always a good idea. Keep up to date on company news and innovations.

GO SMART ... Attracting Positive Attention

1. Identify three ways you can attract some positive attention
   a) at school by your teacher,
   b) at work by your supervisor, and
   c) at home by your parents/guardians.

2. Gil wants to get hired by a local veterinary clinic but he is not sure how to initiate the conversation with the owner. He wants to show the owner he has lots of initiative and would do a great job. Give him some tips on what he might say to the owner to get the conversation started.

Into the Future

Most people will have between seven and ten different careers in their lifetime, so keeping your knowledge and skills up to date can definitely give you the edge when competing for a job. Employers want people with experience and skills, so the more you learn, the more valuable your skills will be to an employer.

How will you keep your knowledge and skills up to date to be able to compete in the world of work? The answer is through education! Here are some educational opportunities that you can research to gain more employability skills.

DO THE SEARCH ▶

Read the Summary on page 151. Are there any ideas you are unsure of? Are there any skills you need to practise? If so, go back and review them.

Educational Opportunities to Increase Employability Skills

Continuing Education—High school credit night school and summer school courses

Virtual School—High school credit courses online

On-the-Job Training—Opportunities for training in the workplace offered by the employer

Conferences and Workshops—Seminars and workshops in your area of interest

Community-Based Education—Credit programs that integrate classroom theory with practical experience in the workplace. Based on a partnership between the school and a business or community organization. Involves the participation of students, teachers, and placement supervisors.

Job Shadowing—Opportunities to spend time observing different roles and responsibilities in the workplace

Volunteering—Donation of time and skills to a business or community organization

Exchange Programs—Programs and courses that allow you to learn another language and culture outside your country

General Interest Courses—Courses based on interests such as painting, canoeing, computers, languages, dancing, cooking, and so forth

Specialized Training Courses—Specialized literacy or numeracy courses

 **... Educational Opportunities**

Create a brochure to explain to Grade 9 students who are new to high school three of the programs listed in the Educational Opportunities to Increase Employability Skills chart. Your teacher will provide you with links needed for this research.

◀ **DO THE SEARCH**

This chapter introduced you to the following ideas:

1. First impressions are always important—especially in the world of work!

2. Plan carefully for your first day on the job: arrive on time and prepared, know what is expected of you, and ask a lot of good questions.

3. Essential skills are crucial in the world of work: reading, document use, numeracy, writing, oral communication, working with others, thinking, computer use, and continuous learning will take you far in whatever field you choose to get into.

4. Interpersonal skills such as negotiating and dealing with difficult conversations often go unmentioned, but they are key to creating a successful work environment for yourself and others.

5. Making mistakes is inevitable. Managing your mistakes is an art form!

6. Character traits that can enhance your work experiences include: responsibility, respect, honesty and integrity, initiative, and seeking out opportunity.

7. Finding strategies to make the most out of your work experiences will benefit you in the short term and in the long term. Do a good job. Be a team player.

8. Whether it be through in-house training programs, online courses, or volunteering, continuous learning will benefit you in your chosen career.

Confident that you are ready to move forward?
Then go to the next chapter.

151

PART 4

LOOKING BEYOND

In this part of *Work Smart*, you will have the opportunity to

- apply your *Work Smart* knowledge and skills to a variety of Career Studies situations
- imagine yourself in the future—who will you be and how did you get there?

12

"What's next?" you may be asking. Now that you've learned more about yourself and your career opportunities, it's time to apply your knowledge and skills in a few situations and demonstrate what you can do.

Select one or more of the following activities to do. Before making your selection, read through all the activities once.

When you see the symbol, it means this is a key area to ask for help or feedback.

What do you care about? Helping to protect the environment, your part-time job, the band you play in, doing well at school? In your Career Studies course you learned how these interests and activities could translate into a future career.

Keep Tools 1, 2, and 3 handy while you choose a culminating activity. If you discover more information about yourself by doing this activity, add that information to the appropriate tool.

A Day in the Life

For this activity, make sure you have access to the three Tools that you used throughout the course.

WHY AM I DOING THIS?

In this activity, you will show that you can identify a variety of personal characteristics such as personality, interests, skills, and learning styles in order to answer the question, "Who am I?" You will show that you know how to discover important details about a variety of occupations and post-secondary options, and are able to recognize good-fit and bad-fit career decisions.

WHAT WILL BE THE FINAL PRODUCT OF MY WORK?

You will interview three well-chosen people in order to produce *one* of the following:

- a video
- a diary
- a Facebook page
- a web page
- a PowerPoint presentation
- something else that you negotiate with your teacher.

HOW WILL I DO THIS?

There are several steps you will need to take to make this project manageable.

1. Read each step carefully and make sure you understand how to do it.
2. Set a deadline for each step and write it in your agenda.
3. Get feedback from someone you trust after each step.
4. Ask your teacher for help when you need it.

Your best information and advice on a possible career choice comes from someone who is already doing it.

THE STEPS

1. a) Do a web search for Career Cruising. In the Explore Careers section, choose a field of work to investigate.

   b) Choose a few occupations to look at more closely.

   c) For each of these occupations, review the information and interview sections. Review research skills in Chapter 3 if you need to.

      - Architecture and construction
      - Arts and culture
      - Business and finance
      - Computers and telecommunications
      - Education and social services
      - Fashion and design
      - Law and government
      - Medical and health
      - Natural resources and transportation
      - Science and engineering
      - Skilled trades
      - Services industry
      - Sports and recreation

2. Prepare interview questions to help you answer the following in your final product.

   a) What is a typical day in the life of the person you interviewed?

   b) Describe his or her career pathway, starting from high school.

   c) How would you describe this person's pattern of passions, preferences, and smarts? (Refer to Tool 1 and the terms defined on page 24 of Chapter 2.)

   d) Did your chosen person consider many different fields of work and possible occupations when making his or her career decisions? Explain. (Go back to Chapter 3 for information on decision making.)

   e) Did your chosen person consider all of the post-secondary pathways available when making his or her career decisions? Explain. (Refer to Chapters 4 through 7.)

   f) Is the current occupation of your chosen person a good fit for him or her? (Refer to your Tools and Chapter 3.)

   g) Considering all of the different aspects of this person's life journey, to what degree do you think he or she has found personal satisfaction or has found his or her calling in his or her chosen career? (Refer to Chapter 1.)

3. Write each interview question on a separate index card.

4. Find one person who works in this field to interview.

   a) Use your network. (See Chapter 4.)

   b) Use your cold-calling skills. (See Chapter 4.)

5. Conduct the interview.

   a) Videotape the interview if you want a video as your final product.

   b) Record answers on index cards, regardless of your final product.

6. Do some additional thinking and research to help you answer the following in your final product.

   a) Name occupations in your interviewee's field of work that require *different* post-secondary pathways from the one required by his or her current occupation.

   b) Do you think one of these occupations would be a good fit for the person you are interviewing? Explain.

   c) What should your interviewee consider about the changing world of work when making future career decisions? (Refer to Chapter 1.)

7. Organize your information.

   a) Use index cards or large sticky notes to record separate pieces of information. For example, one answer to an interview question would be one piece.

   b) Use the checklists from Steps 2 and 6 to create headings.

   c) Group individual pieces of information (cards or notes) under the appropriate headings.

8. Choose the best way to present your information. (See What Will Be the Final Product of My Work? on page 154.)

9. Prepare your final product.

   a) Does your product address each of the items from Steps 2 and 6?

   b) Is the information presented in an organized way that is easy to understand?

   c) Is the information presented in a creative way that makes it interesting?

10. Submit your assignment on time and celebrate—you're done!

Star of Your Own Life ... @ Age 30

In this activity, you tell your life story up to the age of 30 by making it into a video.

WHY AM I DOING THIS?

This activity is all about gathering your learning in this course—about yourself and how you fit into the changing world of work—and putting it into a creative media message for your peers, teacher, and family.

Making a video by looking at a future point in time—that is, when you are 30 years old, and then "mapping backward" to how you got there—challenges you to understand your own unique career journey. You will get to consider the decisions you will make because of

- what you value
- what interests drive your choices
- how your learning today may actually be reflected in the jobs you take and dreams you fulfill.

WHAT WILL BE THE FINAL PRODUCT OF MY WORK?

You will create a two- to five-minute digital video. Alternatively, you could make a video blog or PowerPoint presentation. Your life story up to age 30 may be presented as a drama, an interview, a documentary, or another genre of your choice. For this activity, you must complete all three phases: pre-production, production, and post-production.

HOW WILL I DO THIS?

Planning is part of the creative process, the life process, and the career development process. Carefully read and follow the steps: pre-production, production, and post-production. These are guideposts along the way to your finished video.

Don't forget to use your Tools and the information in your portfolio to help make your video a reflection of who you are becoming, what career(s) you are considering, and what dreams you are going to make a reality.

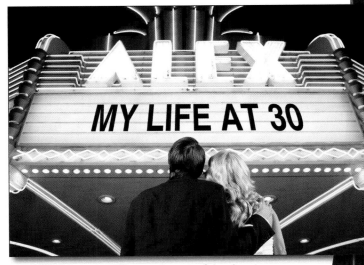

Your life—your career. You are the star of the show!

THE STEPS

1. Plan your pre-production (50 percent of your time).

   a) Brainstorm events and decisions that could have led you to your great life at age 30. Use the graphic organizer provided by your teacher and the visualization questions in Chapter 2, Go Smart, page 21. Open up your portfolio to discover more information about what your dream life at 30 might look like, sound like, and feel like. Take a deep breath. Begin to imagine and create how you got there.

   b) Decide on five main events and/or decisions. Use your portfolio and Tools for information about your passions, preferences, and smarts and career opportunities today and tomorrow.

   c) Generate details around these main events using the "5 W's and How." Ask classmates, friends, and family for their ideas.

   d) Plan the audio portion of the video. This is everything the audience will hear, and includes background music, sound effects, and dialogue.

   e) Plan the video portion of the video. This is everything the audience will see, and includes location choices, extras, props, wardrobe and make-up, camera shots (from wide to close-up), and camera angles.

   f) Place your five main ideas (decisions or events, or a combination thereof) and arrange them into a beginning, middle, and end—not necessarily in that order. You could, for example, start the story at age 30 and work backward.

   g) Write your script—two to three typed pages. Your script is the back-bone of your story or documentary.

storyboard
graphic organizer to show all the visual frames (action, dialogue, camera shots) in a script

   h) Create a **storyboard**—the key tool for any video or filmmaker.

Five Steps to Creating a Storyboard

- Using index cards or sticky notes, sketch one main idea and details, including the camera shot, on each card from the written script.
- Arrange the index cards to reflect your story.
- Number the cards in order to shoot the video.
- Add the dialogue or monologue you want to each card.
- Make a master storyboard to see the overall story; make photocopies or e-versions if others are helping you with this activity.

   i) Now you're ready to cast your video and rehearse!

2. Shoot your video (20 percent of your time).

   a) Gather your equipment:

- digital camcorder or video camera
- tripod
- batteries and charger
- lights and stand (if possible)
- lapel or hand-held microphone (if possible).

   b) Set up your equipment about an hour before shooting. Make sure your props and clothing make the scenes realistic 15 years down the road.

   c) Experiment with your camera shots. A wide shot usually focuses on the character from head to toe, and is good for introducing a person or situation. A medium shot is a closer shot that shows detail of the characters. A close-up shows the character's facial features and can create an interesting dramatic effect.

   d) Experiment with your camera angles. A high-angle shot involves holding the camera high so that the character looks small. With a low-angle shot the camera is held low; the character usually looks important to the story. A cut-away shot cuts away from the main action. A cut-in shot cuts into the scene and focuses closely on the character's action.

3. Do your post-production (30 percent of your time).

   a) Download your footage onto your home computer, or your school computer, if permitted. Ask for assistance.

   b) Begin to edit the best shots and footage of your life story.

   c) Add sound. You could use a program such as Audacity, free, easy-to-use audio-editing and recording software.

   d) Locate some editing tips online related to your specific equipment. Be brave, experiment, collaborate with friends and classmates, and have fun!

DO THE SEARCH

   e) Check that your final product is organized, entertaining, and easy to understand.

4. Submit your assignment on time and celebrate—you're done!

The Career Path Board Game

This activity involves creating your own career path board game with challenges, rewards, and penalties.

WHY AM I DOING THIS?

Creating a board game lets you demonstrate your mastery of the knowledge and skills involved in the career journey. In your game, you will outline the steps of the career journey and reward or penalize players for knowing or not knowing some career essentials.

WHAT WILL BE THE FINAL PRODUCT OF MY WORK?

Your board game should include

- a board with spaces to land on and a career destination—that is, the end of the journey (the first player to get there wins)
- a brief how-to-play guide
- Knowledge Challenge! cards
- Skills Challenge! cards
- player pieces
- dice or spinner.

HOW WILL I DO THIS?

Initially, you will just need *Work Smart* and index cards. Once you have created the content for the game, you can physically design a board and format the Knowledge Challenge! and Skills Challenge! cards as well as your how-to guide on a computer if you wish. Follow the steps carefully for the best results.

THE STEPS

1. Plot out the career journey on your index cards.
   a) Decide how many squares you should have on your board in total. Tip: Lots of board games have about 35–40 squares along the perimeter. Initially, you can lay your index cards out in the shape of a board.
   b) Remember that each square represents one step on the career journey, so select carefully. As you fill these in, you must demonstrate that you understand these steps. Include the most important information.
   c) Every two squares, include a Knowledge Challenge! or Skills Challenge! Write Knowledge Challenge! or Skills Challenge! on the board square and create a separate deck of cards for each type of challenge. (You will write these challenges in the next step.) These decks can be kept in the middle of the finished board.

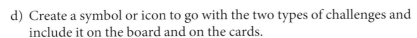

d) Create a symbol or icon to go with the two types of challenges and include it on the board and on the cards.

Here's what the first four squares of your board might look like.

Your career journey starts with knowing your passions, preferences, and smarts.	Your actions today, along with your dreams and goals, show something important about your career path.	**Knowledge Challenge!** 	Making mistakes along the way is OK because it's part of growing.

2. Create your Knowledge Challenge! and Skills Challenge! cards.

- A Knowledge Challenge! should be a question that relates to an important idea. You can find these ideas by examining the summaries of each chapter of *Work Smart*, by reviewing the main headings of the chapters and skimming the information, and by looking in your portfolio.

- A Skills Challenge! should be a question that asks the player what he or she would *do* in a situation or how he or she would do it. Get ideas for these challenges by reviewing the Go Smart activities and Real-Time Resumé and Career Coach features in each chapter of *Work Smart*.

EXAMPLE

Skills Challenge!

How would you demonstrate that you are able to handle responsibility and more adult privileges?

You can find this information in Chapter 3 in the main text and in the Career Coach feature.

On your index cards, make sure to note where the *answer* to that Skills Challenge! can be found in *Work Smart*. Summarize that information.

Driving your parents' car with safety and consideration for everyone—that's one common way to demonstrate that you can handle responsibility and adult privileges.

3. Decide what your rewards and penalties will be.

a) What will failing or succeeding at a challenge mean for players? You could send them forward or backward several squares. Or you could let them miss the next challenge or take an extra challenge. Use your imagination!

b) Write down your penalties to include as rules in your how-to guide.

4. Create your how-to guide for playing the game.

a) List and number the steps for playing the game.

b) List your rules for playing the game, including rewards and penalties.

5. Design your board and cards.

a) Use poster board or heavy cardboard for your final game board and print your challenge cards on card stock. Make sure your how-to guide is on a neat sheet of paper.

6. Check your final product.

a) Does your product address each of the items from Steps 1–4?

b) Have you included answers to the challenges for your teacher to read?

c) Is your board game presented in an organized way that is easy to understand?

7. Submit your assignment on time and celebrate—you're done!

A

abilities
something you do naturally; your talents and aptitudes—e.g., singing, running, using numbers or languages easily

adrenaline
hormone secreted by the body to help it deal with physical or emotional stress

advocates
people who speak up for a cause, for others, or for themselves

anecdote
short account of an interesting incident

apprentice
someone learning a new trade or skill (from a journeyperson)

apprenticeship program
post-secondary education required to become a skilled professional

aspirations
strong desire to achieve something great; your goals and dreams mixed into one

attitude
way of thinking and feeling about something or someone that shows your true opinion

B

baby boomers
people who were born during the post–World War II baby boom between 1946 and the early 1960s

Bachelor's degree
first-level university degree (e.g., a Bachelor of Arts or of Science) in any discipline; below a Master's degree

benefits
services provided by an employer in addition to wages, such as life insurance or drug and dental plans

bursary
award of money, usually based on financial need, that you do not have to pay back

business cards
small cards with all of your contact information on them

C

career
summary of all your education, paid work, volunteer experiences, and activities of interest to you

certificate
document granted by a college to a student who has completed a specific field of study (e.g., elevator mechanic)

challenges
opportunities to grow and to test abilities in a demanding but exciting way

commission
percentage paid to you of the total amount of merchandise you sell

contract position
employment with set terms (e.g., lasting several months or a year) and set objectives

credit
recognition for successfully completing a course; you need 30 credits to graduate from high school

Credit Counselling Summary
tool used to track courses students have taken and those they need to take in order to graduate

D

degree
title awarded by a university to a student who has completed a program of studies

diploma
document granted by a college to show academic achievement in a particular field of study

GLOSSARY

Doctor of Philosophy (PhD)
university degree ranking above a Master's degree (in any discipline), involving original research and a thesis

E

e-folio
electronic portfolio; an e-folio is a great way to save your work and update it frequently in cyberspace

employee manual
company handbook that explains a company's policies and practices with respect to employees—e.g., dress code, office behaviour, and Internet access

employee training session
period of time devoted to training employees for specific aspects of their job

essential skills
skills that are essential because they are the basis of all other skills

extrovert
how you get energy; an extrovert recharges by being around people and having conversations

F

flat fee
set amount of money charged for services rendered

flexible hours
work hours outside the typical 9–5 workday

freelance
selling your work to a company or organization for an agreed-on rate

G

GDP
gross domestic product; the value of domestically produced goods or services in one year

global citizenship
belief that all citizens of the world are responsible for each other and for the planet

goals
what you want to achieve for yourself

grant
award of money, usually based on financial need, that you do not have to pay back

gross pay
pay before expenses or taxes have been deducted

H

habit
something you have gotten used to doing without thinking

I

influences
anything or anyone that contributes to the way you think, and challenges or supports the decisions you make

initiative
ability to take action without being prompted by someone else

interests
what you like; something that attracts you—e.g., a book, a film, a superhero, an issue

introvert
how you get energy; an introvert recharges by being alone and reflecting quietly

J

job
position that has specific tasks and duties at a specific location

job fairs
events where employers display available jobs, accept resumés, and interview on the spot

journeyperson
someone who is experienced and certified in a particular skilled profession

L

longitudinal
repeated observation or examination of a set of subjects and variables over time

M

Master's degree
university degree ranking above a Bachelor's degree (in any discipline)

N

net pay
pay after expenses and taxes have been deducted

non-governmental organization (NGO)
non-profit group that works on a specific cause that is not funded or managed by the government (e.g., the World Wildlife Fund)

O

occupation
general title given to a group of similar work roles and skills (e.g., engineers)

opportunity
favourable situation or chance to do something

options
courses you can choose to take; these courses are not mandatory to graduate from high school

P

personality
your "self" that you build over time; the total of your physical, mental, emotional, and social characteristics

personal management
organizing, directing, and controlling yourself and your own behaviour

physiological
referring to an organism's (in this case, a person's) normal or typical functioning

portfolio
tool used to organize and maintain personal, academic, and/or career-related credentials and evidence of accomplishments

prerequisites
courses you need to take and pass before enrolling in other courses

R

recruiting companies
businesses that are paid by other companies to find them potential employees

required courses
courses you need to take and pass in order to graduate

respect
treating something or someone with consideration and thoughtfulness

resumé
summary of all of your education, job, volunteer and other accomplishments and experiences; a resumé is often called a curriculum vitæ or a C.V.

S

scholarship
award of money, based on academic merit or other factors, that you do not have to pay back

sector share
a sector is one part of the economy that produces revenue; a sector share of the GDP refers to how much money of the total GDP that sector makes

sectors
categories of different kinds of work activity

severance pay
payment made to a terminated employee

skilled professions
occupations requiring expertise in using specific, hands-on skills and related knowledge, gained through an apprenticeship program

GLOSSARY

skills
something you have learned or studied—e.g., playing the piano, speaking another language, leading a group discussion, using a computer

Social Insurance Number
government-issued number identifying one who is allowed to work in Canada

storyboard
graphic organizer to show all the visual frames (action, dialogue, camera shots) in a script

subcontracted
assigned to someone else to do

symptom
sign or indication of something

T

temporary positions
jobs that are available for a limited time

transferable skills
skills acquired in any area of life that can be applied to other situations, including a job

U

unconventional
out of the ordinary

undergraduate studies
studies pursued by students at a university who have not yet earned a degree

union
group of employees that negotiates with an employer about wages, benefits, and opportunities

V

values
your core beliefs; what drives you

venture capital
money invested to grow or expand a business

vulnerable
with your defences down; as though you could be attacked

Y

yin and yang
in Chinese philosophy, two opposing but complementary forces in the universe

CREDITS

Legend: t = top; b = bottom; c = centre; l = left; r = right.